1 Week I

s book is due f   ...   te shown below.

The Arnold and Caroline Rose Monograph Series
of the American Sociological Association

Tasks and social relationships in classrooms

A study of instructional organization and its consequences

Other books in the series

J. Milton Yinger, Kiyoshi Ikeda, Frank Laycock, and Stephen J. Cutler: *Middle Start: An Experiment in the Educational Enrichment of Young Adolescents*

James A. Geschwender: *Class, Race, and Worker Insurgency: The League of Revolutionary Black Workers*

Paul Ritterband: *Education, Employment, and Migration: Israel in Comparative Perspective*

John Low-Beer: *Protest and Participation: The New Working Class in Italy*

Orrin E. Klapp: *Opening and Closing: Strategies of Information Adaptation in Society*

Rita James Simon: *Continuity and Change: A Study of Two Ethnic Communities in Israel*

Marshall B. Clinard: *Cities with Little Crime: The Case of Switzerland*

David R. Heise: *Understanding Events: Affect and the Construction of Social Action*

Richard E. Johnson: *Juvenile Delinquency and its Origins: An Integrated Theoretical Approach*

Volumes previously published by the American Sociological Association

Michael Schwartz and Sheldon Stryker: *Deviance, Selves and Others*

Robert M. Hauser: *Socioeconomic Background and Educational Performance*

Morris Rosenberg and Roberta G. Simmons: *Black and White Self-Esteem: The Urban School Child*

Chad Gordon: *Looking Ahead: Self-Conceptions: Race and Family as Determinants of Adolescent Orientation to Achievement*

Anthony M. Orum: *Black Students in Protest: A Study in the Origins of the Black Student Movement*

Ruth M. Gasson, Archibald O. Haller, and William H. Sewell: *Attitudes and Facilitation in the Attainment of Status*

Sheila R. Klatsky: *Patterns of Contact with Relatives*

Herman Turk: *Interorganizational Activation in Urban Communities: Deductions from the Concepts of System*

John DeLamater: *The Study of Political Commitment*

Alan C. Kerckhoff: *Ambition and Attainment: A Study of Four Samples of American Boys*

Scott McNall: *The Greek Peasant*

Lowell L. Hargens: *Patterns of Scientific Research: A Comparative Analysis of Research in Three Scientific Fields*

Charles Hirschman: *Ethnic Stratification in Peninsular Malaysia*

Tasks and social relationships in classrooms

A study of instructional organization and its consequences

Steven T. Bossert

Assistant Professor of Sociology
The University of Michigan

Cambridge University Press

Cambridge
London   New York   Melbourne

Published by the Syndics of the Cambridge University Press
The Pitt Building, Trumpington Street, Cambridge CB2 1RP
Bentley House, 200 Euston Road, London NW1 2DB
32 East 57th Street, New York, NY 10022, USA
296 Beaconsfield Parade, Middle Park, Melbourne 3206, Australia

First Published 1979

Printed in the United States of America
Typeset by Jay's Publishers Services Inc., North Scituate, Mass.
Printed and bound by The Murray Printing Company, Westford, Mass.

Library of Congress Cataloging in Publication Data

Bossert, Steven T. 1948–
Tasks and social relationships in classrooms.

(The Arnold and Caroline Rose monograph series
of the American Sociological Association)

Bibliography: p.

1. Teaching. 2. Interaction
analysis in education. 3. Classroom management.
I. Title. II. Series: The Arnold and Caroline Rose
monograph series in sociology.
LB1025.2.B675   371.1'02   78-67260
ISBN 0 521 22445 4   hard covers
ISBN 0 521 29505 X paperback

Contents

vi   Contents

Tables

Preface

The search for school effects has not been particularly fruitful for educational researchers. Schooling environments have been described alternatively as structures of resources, roles, expectations, values, and verbal exchanges; yet variations in these properties have not been determinately linked to students' achievements, attitudes, normative orientations, or behavior patterns. The failure to relate structural properties of schools and classrooms to what students and teachers actually do has resulted, in part, from simplistic, input-output and "black box" research designs typically used to study schools. These do not capture the complexity of the schooling environment or illuminate the processes of education. However, even when everyday interactions in schools and classrooms are examined directly, models of classroom interaction generally suffer from the assumption that teacher personality or expectations are the primary determiners of classroom behavior and that classroom structure can be characterized as a system of dyadic exchanges between teacher and pupils. These views ignore the collective properties of instruction and the effects these may have on teacher-pupil and peer relations.

The research reported in this book rests on the simple observation that it is within the context of daily activities that teacher and students make judgments about themselves and others, interact and form social ties, and experience social sanctions. The study was designed to examine how the structure of activities, particularly the nature of common, recurrent instructional tasks, shape both teacher and pupil behavior. Extensive observations of several elementary school classrooms and interviews with teachers and pupils provide an in-depth look at how variations in certain forms of instruction affect a teacher's use of individualized versus formalized controls, the allocation of instructional assistance among pupils, the formation of children's friendship ties and peer groups, and the development of norms of group competition and cooperation.

Chapter 1 presents the perspective guiding the research. It differs from traditional treatments of classroom structure and draws on concepts from small group and industrial work studies to characterize the social organization of instruction and its consequences for interpersonal interaction. Chapter 2 describes the study design and its rationale. Of particular note is the longitudinal and comparative nature of the research in which a subgroup of children was observed for two school years. This enables concrete comparisons to be made among teachers and among children who experienced similar and different classroom organizations, effectively controlling for personal characteristics to illuminate structural effects. Chapter 3 provides a descriptive ethnography of four of the classrooms studied. It gives a "natural history" of events without attempting to categorize or analyze the nature of classroom structure. Chapter 4 examines the teacher-pupil relationship in detail. The effects of different instructional organizations on group management, the exercise of control, and the allocation of special instructional assistance are analyzed in the light of competing personality and organizational explanations of teacher behavior. Chapter 5 describes the consequences of classroom structure for peer relations. How pupil peer groupings formed and changed throughout the school year and how academic performance played a different role in shaping friendship ties in the different classrooms demonstrate the way in which the structure of activities shapes peer competition and cooperation. Chapter 6 is an overview of the relationship between a classroom's instructional organization and patterns of teacher and pupil interaction. A further illustration of the effect of instructional patterns on teacher behavior is provided in case materials that describe one teacher's attempt to change classroom patterns and peer relations during the sixth month of school. The final chapter, Chapter 7, presents some implications of this research for studying the effects of classroom structure on pupil achievement and on normative socialization.

Research on classroom structure is just beginning to develop a detailed picture of the nature and consequences of instructional organization. This analysis of classroom task organizations and of their effect on the development of social relationships discloses some of the contents of the educational "black box" and moves beyond simplistic models of personality and social behavior commonly used in classroom research. The study provides clear conceptual and methodological implications for future research on schooling as well as fruitful ways for educational policy makers and practitioners to view the instructional process.

I am most deeply indebted to Charles Bidwell for his support and encouragement throughout the course of this research and writing. He has the fine ability to help one transform scattered ideas and observations into solid questions and interpretations. Robert Dreeben and Barry Schwartz also played important roles during the research and analysis. Encouragement and helpful criticism were received from David Street, Richard White, Benjamin Hodgkins, and William Rodak, and I am grateful for their insights and understanding.

This research would not have been possible without the openness and patience of the teachers, staff, children, and parents at Harper School. The findings reported in this study do not reflect all that I learned from them.

Kathleen Vargo, Margaret Grillot, and Billie Norris were invaluable in the preparation of this manuscript.

S.T.B.

1. Introduction

It is almost trite to say that schooling is a process of social interaction. Recognition of the intimate link between learning processes and social relationships permeates both the popular literature and the scholarly research on education. Images of the good teacher abound as do prescriptions for establishing proper classroom social relations. Yet our understanding of classroom processes is extremely limited despite numerous studies of teacher style, peer relations in school, and classroom climate. Besides failing clearly to relate classroom or teacher differences to pupil behavior, research on schooling has overlooked the influence of certain classroom structural properties on both the teacher and pupil behavior. If learning occurs within the context of social relationships that develop within a classroom, then the forces that pattern interaction between teacher and pupil and among peers are fundamental to the study of schooling processes.

This book concerns some of the consequences of classroom organization, particularly the analysis of structures that characterize differences between classrooms. Its major premise rests on the observation that the daily activities in which individuals engage play an important role in shaping the development of their social relationships: As teacher and pupils interact within the context of recurrent classroom activities, patterns of interaction emerge and particular social relationships develop. To the extent that classrooms employ different activity structures, different interaction patterns should emerge. This view differs from the usual highly individualistic conceptions of classroom processes in which characteristics of individuals are seen as the primary determiners of behavior, and instead focuses on the social organization of the learning environment as a frame for emerging social interaction. The research reported here examines the nature of classroom activities, particularly those elements that constitute differences in activity types, and the consequences of various classroom activity organizations for patterns of interaction that develop between teacher and pupil and

1

among pupils. That is, it explores the linkages between classroom activity organizations and the social relationships that emerge within them.

Several sociologists have noted the importance of studying the factors that shape social relationships in schools and other socialization settings. In a seminal essay on the structural properties of people-processing institutions, Wheeler (1966) contends that the psychological outcomes of socialization result from the recurrent conditions in which members interact and that these conditions themselves are set by basic organizational properties. Forms of social relationships, from which social norms are acquired, derive from the structural characteristics of the institution. Wheeler indicates that differences among organizations in their goals, the composition and processing of their members, and their relationships to the external environment lead to differences in the socialization experiences of their members. Although Wheeler's paper clearly indicates the potential value of studying the structural conditions that shape socialization experiences, this has not been done. Except for Street, Vinter, and Perrow's (1966) study of the organizational goals and technologies of different correctional institutions, the empirical examination of the relationships among organizational factors, social relationships, and socialization outcomes has not developed.

Dreeben (1968), however, has applied this idea theoretically to the school in comparing its organization and socialization outcomes to those of the family. He contends that what children learn derives from the nature of their experiences and that different experiences develop in settings characterized by different organizational arrangements. Because the family and the school, as social institutions, differ in terms of the boundaries and size of social groupings, the duration of social relationships, the relative number of adults to nonadults, the degree of homogeneity in members' social characteristics, and the extent to which members can observe one another's behavior, they provide different tasks, constraints, and opportunities for interaction. These, in turn, influence the norms children learn within these settings. For example, independence learning is fostered by

the fact that school children are removed from persons with whom they have already formed strong relationships of dependency, and the sheer size of a classroom assemblage limits each pupil's claim to personal contact with the teacher, and more so at the secondary levels than at the elementary. This numerical property of classrooms reduces pupils' opportunities for establishing new relationships of dependency with adults and for receiving help from them [Dreeben, 1968, p. 67].

Dreeben, then, argues that the structural properties of schools create tasks and situations in which children are more likely to learn certain norms than if they had remained only within the family unit. Norm learning occurs within the context of recurrent activities; therefore, the organizational factors shaping these activities and their attendant social relationships are central to the study of schooling.

In a review of moral socialization and schooling, Bidwell (1972) has labeled Dreeben's analysis of schooling effects as the "activity structures" approach. Following this perspective, Bidwell argues that characteristic school activities exemplify moral principles or, at least, give moral meaning to required behavior. The moral meaning of acts derives from the "social organization of the school as it structures opportunities for interpersonal and within-classroom-group comparisons" (Bidwell, 1972, p. 20). Social control attempts, for example, can be either heightened or weakened depending on the character of the relationships between teacher and pupil and of group identifications within peer networks. Learning moral principles occurs within the context of developing social relationships. In fact, Bidwell speculates that

learning commitments to forms of social relations will be more effective if it occurs through activity structure than through influence or identification (though the latter mechanisms are not without power to alter such commitments); the acquisition of such commitments requires the concrete manifestations of the rewarding qualities of a given form of social relation that an appropriate activity structure and its attendant sanctions can provide. Learning *commitments to moral orientations* may be more protean, occurring either by generalization from experience in activity structures or more explicitly through some form of social control [Bidwell, 1972, p. 25; emphasis in the original].

According to this perspective, socialization settings that differ in their characteristic activities and social relationships also should differ in the norms learned by members. The organizational properties of the setting, as they shape activities and patterns of interaction, are elemental to the learning process.

Although the importance of activity structures and social relationships is well recognized, these examinations of the organizational properties of socialization settings have focused on differences among institutions. Wheeler examines variations among prisons, schools, and mental hospitals, and Dreeben analyzes factors that differentiate the family and the school. Yet subsettings within an organization also differ in their organizational properties and in the social relationships that emerge. Within schools, for example, classroom organizations may vary substantially. The popular conceptions of "traditional" versus "open" classrooms express perceived differences in classroom social organization, differences that (theoretically) may affect the development of social relationships and learning outcomes. However, the variables characterizing differences among institutions cannot adequately distinguish many of the differences among subsettings within one institution. Even though subsettings are likely to share general organizational goals and similar problems in relation to the external environment as well as have comparable procedures for ordering membership composition, subsettings may differ considerably in their activity structures and the patterns of interpersonal relations that develop within them. Most classrooms, for example, share the institutional goals of moral and technical socialization, deal similarly with intrusions from parents and community members, and contain children who are ordered by age and mixed by sex and other social characteristics. Also, classrooms do not vary substantially in terms of the factors Dreeben uses to characterize differences between family and school: These institutional-level factors were not intended to differentiate classroom structures. How, then, do classrooms, as organizational subsettings, differ? In accepting the viability of Wheeler's, Dreeben's, and Bidwell's general formulations, the identification of factors that distinguish among classrooms, particularly as these shape differences in interpersonal relations and daily recurrent activities, becomes an important topic for investigation.

Although it is beyond the scope of this research to examine the socialization consequences of identifiable classroom differences, the study of activity structures and their associated patterns of social relations should provide some implications for examining schooling effects. After all, learning is a social process – its outcomes being influenced by its form of social organization. Examining the organizational bases of classroom activities and interaction constitutes a first step in the study of learning outcomes.

Work and social relationships

The relationship between task activities and intragroup relations is not a new idea; sociologists who study industrial work settings and other task groups have long recognized its importance. There are numerous illustrations of the notion that the "scheme of activities" will affect the "scheme of interaction" among group members. Homans (1950), for example, has shown that the organization of tasks exerts considerable influence over the nature of the relationships that develop among workers. In his observations of the Bank Wiring Room, Homans noted that clique formation reflected the patterns of interaction that occurred during work. Those men who were stationed next to one another or worked on the same piece of wiring (a wireman and a solderman) were most likely to talk informally and play games during rest and lunch periods. Likewise, Borgatta and Bales (1953) have shown that patterns of interaction among members in small experimental task groups develop in response to the type of task performed by group members.

In analyzing the effect of work situations on group relations, several crucial variables have been discovered. Sayles (1958, p. 42) found that "the internal structuring of work operations . . . affects significantly the behavior characteristics of a group. That is, the relations between members prescribed by the flow of work processes are a critical variable shaping the internal social systems of a group." In studying the responses of industrial work groups to grievance procedures and their propensity to strike, Sayles analyzed several factory settings in terms of the size of the work group, the essentialness of the group's function within the organization, and the extent of worker responsibility for judgment in completing tasks. These variables account for differences in group cohesion, interdependence among members, and the propensity for group action.

Central to Sayles's analysis was the division of labor within the group. Where the division of labor was high, for example, where there was the separation or elimination of workers doing identical tasks, members tended not to engage in concerted group activity: They were less likely to participate as a collectivity in union organizing and grievance procedures than members of groups in which workers completed a common task in a single area. Sayles attributed this to the fact that when workers are separated and/or performing different tasks, they are not able to interact freely with fellow workers: ". . . intrinsic personality characteristics are less the determining factor of whom the worker talks to, when, and how often, than the work process which requires that he spend more time with some people than with others, and may actually specify his entire interaction pattern [within the work group] " (p. 74).

Worker relations are not the only patterns of interaction affected by the structure of the work process. Woodward (1958) demonstrates how management-worker relations are influenced by the nature of the product manufactured. Her analysis of the effects of differing technologies on industrial relations shows that less conflict develops between supervisor and subordinate in process and unit production than in mass production settings. This suggests that certain characteristics distinguishing industrial technologies, such as the division of labor and the extent of worker responsibility over the task, also influence supervisory-subordinate relations.

In addition to the structure of the task itself, the method of evaluation is another important element of the organization of work, and many studies have examined the impact of supervision on work group relations. In one, Blau (1955) found that evaluation procedures comparing the productivity of group members decreased the amount of social cohesion in the work group. In the state agency he studied, the posting of output statistics for each counselor in the office created a highly competitive situation in which counselors vied for interviewees and hoarded job openings. The resulting competition produced weak social cohesion among counselors, curtailed lunchtime association, and inhibited the flow of advice within the group. By contrast, in another agency where agents were assigned to cases and evaluated individually, lunchtime association and advice were frequent even though the latter was proscribed.

In examining task evaluation systems, two important dimensions arise – the extent of differential rewarding, and the interdependence of task performance. For example, Miller and Hamblin's (1963) study of work group productivity found that high levels of competition among workers developed where individual performance was rewarded differentially and task performance depended partly on the cooperation of co-workers. When individual performance was rewarded differentially but task performance was independent of fellow workers, competition was less intense than in the interdependence situation. Moreover, it is generally known that status systems emerge when individual rewards are affected by other group members (Thibaut and Kelly, 1959). Evaluation procedures that allow for individual comparisons and make rewards contingent on comparative assessments of performance foster the development of competitive status systems within a work group. When the demands of work are instrumental and clearly linked to a competitive reward structure, status within a group and interpersonal bonding will depend on individual performance. The competition that results decreases group cohesion, making salient only those courses of action and social relationships that increase a worker's productivity and, hence, his chances of obtaining rewards. In settings that do not promote individual competition, group members are free to establish a variety of social contacts without regard for their instrumental value in securing performance rewards. But workers may organize informally to restrict competitive relations even when the method of evaluation rewards workers' performances differentially (Roy, 1952).

The structure of task activities and their associated evaluation mechanisms are important factors shaping the development of social relations within a group. Patterns of interaction among work group members and between supervisor and workers are influenced by factors such as the size of the work group, its division of labor, the amount of worker responsibility over his task, and the methods of evaluating and rewarding task performance. Unfortunately, the analysis of work organization has not extended beyond the study of industrial work units and experimental task groups. Except in a few studies, like Shils's (1950) examination of wartime and peacetime armies and Breton's (1973) analysis of community structure and work organization, the structure of task activities and its consequences for social relationships have not been detailed for many different types of groups.

Classrooms and task organization

Classrooms are places where teachers and pupils work; however, few studies of classroom differences or schooling outcomes have examined the consequences of distinctive types of work organizations, or activity structures, for the emergence of social relationships within classrooms. Even though a massive body of literature has been generated on the sociometric structure of a classroom and the effects of teacher style, we know little about the variable conditions under which interactions occur and social relationships form.

The sociometric tradition of classroom research has focused on the relationship between pupil background characteristics, such as social class, and peer group networks. Research has shown that children often choose friends within their own socioeconomic status group and that this tends to reinforce existing differences in educational aspirations among these groups (Neugarten, 1942; Dahlke, 1953; Lippitt and Gold, 1959). Other studies have attempted to examine how particular sociometric patterns within a classroom or a school affect pupil achievement and self-concept (Grolund, 1953; Grann, 1956; Schmuck, 1962). It has been argued that a classroom with "good" sociometric structure will promote statisfying intragroup relations and, hence, create high levels of individual motivation for achievement and group performance; the characteristics of "good" sociometric structure are high rates of inter-personal contact, a lack of sharp cleavages within the group, the absence of isolated individuals, and strong leadership. These sociometric studies, however, have presented unclear and often contradictory results. Most have not been able to identify significant associations between socio-metric structure and pupil learning. Moreover, they have overlooked the possible effects that certain structural properties of the learning environ-ment may have on the development of peer networks, either in influ-encing friendship choices within social class groupings or in reinforcing segregation between various friendship groups. The emergence of a classroom's sociometric structure is usually attributed to the social and personality characteristics of class members. Yet, as the research on small task groups and industrial work groups has pointed out, structural characteristics such as a group's activity organization and reward system strongly influence group sociometric structure. To understand the rela-tionship between group organization and schooling processes, we must examine the structural arrangements that affect intragroup relations.

The second major tradition in classroom research has been the teacher "style" and "effectiveness" studies. One of the earliest studies attempting to link a teacher's behavior to group patterns was the Iowa research on leadership styles (Lewin et al., 1939; Lippitt and White, 1962). Three styles, authoritarian, democratic, and laissez faire, were found to produce different patterns of interaction, satisfaction, and pro-ductivity among children in task groups. Although this research indi-cated some differences in group patterns – the democratically led group was most satisfied and least aggressive, and the autocratically led group was the most productive as long as the leader was present – the effect of leadership style remains vague: Group differences were small, and it is unclear whether the results from small voluntary play groups can be generalized to classrooms.

This research has stimulated other studies of teacher leadership styles, basically of the extent to which the teacher dominates classroom activities. Flander's (1960) work on teacher influence and Gordon and Adler's (1963) study of teacher leadership are exemplary. Stern (1963), however, has indicated in his review of this research that no consistent results have emerged: About the only conclusions that can be drawn from these studies is that there is no "best" type of teacher (Boocock, 1972).

In addition to their failure to identify clear relationships between teacher differences and pupil behavior, these studies have not examined teacher behavior itself as an emergent phenomenon within the classroom setting. Rather, they view certain teacher characteristics as static preconditions for all subsequent classroom interactions; and they assume that only pupil behavior develops in response to the classroom setting. This perspective obscures the dynamic processes involved in the formation of teacher-pupil relationships as well as the effect that certain structural properties of the setting, like its organization of work, may have on patterns of interaction.

In contrast to traditional classroom studies, research on "behavior settings" has not ignored the relationships between structural properties and patterns of interpersonal behavior in small groups. In a study of four camp activities, Gump and Sutton-Smith (1955) observed children's behavior in six activity settings: sharing, helping, asserting, blocking, demanding, and attacking. They found "the amount and kind of social interaction is significantly affected by variation of activity-settings" (Gump and Sutton-Smith, 1955, p. 756). In other words, they observed different rates of the six behavior categories in the four different camp activities. Gump (1967) later extended his ideas about activity settings to classrooms. There he found relationships among activity patterns, teacher leadership, and pupil involvement in the activity. Gump's research substantiated two earlier attempts to relate classroom activities to pupil and teacher behavior; Kowatrakul (1959) found that the amount of pupil "work involvement" depended on the type of task assigned, and Hughes (1959) found a relationship between task activity and dominative teacher authority.

This research on the consequences of activity settings for teachers' and children's behavior, however, has not analyzed the characteristics of the activity setting itself. In a sense, it presents a tautological argument. Gump and Sutton-Smith argue that children will exhibit cooperative behavior in activities entailing cooperative behavior. Likewise, Hughes finds activities that place the teacher at the center of instruction will produce dominative teacher behavior. No one, though has examined the constitutive elements of task structure, such as the division of labor within the group, the size of the task group, and the method of evaluation used in the classroom, as these shape interpersonal behavior.

Furthermore, the research on "behavior settings" has not examined fully the emergent qualities of pupil and teacher behavior. Although Gump's and Kowatrakul's studies have not assumed that teacher behavior is the central organizing component of classroom interaction, they have not viewed classroom social relationships as developing from the interaction of teacher and pupils within the context of the task structure.[1]

Classroom tasks and social relationships

Many different activities occur in classrooms. Children recite, discuss, read, play, build, and paint. There are times when activities must be carried on independently; times when pupils work together in small groups; and times when the activity involves the entire class. Occasionally, children may choose the task they wish to do, but most often the teacher specifies what is to be done and how. Every classroom activity, though, can be described in terms of its task characteristics. Just as in the analysis of industrial work tasks, classroom task activities[2] vary in the size of the work group (from single pupil to the whole class), the division of labor, that is, the number of different tasks being completed during the same period (from single task for the entire class to individualized instruction) and the interdependence of task performance, and the degree of pupil choice (or teacher dominance) over the task (from total specification by the teacher to full pupil choice). For example, recitation is a common classroom activity usually characterized by full class participation, one member at a time, a single topic and task, and teacher control over topic and pupil participation. By contrast, individualized instruction atomizes the work activity and often involves substantial pupil choice over the topic and method of completion.

Classroom activities also vary in terms of the methods used to evaluate pupils' performances. Although others have indicated that public, comparative judgments are an ever-present fact of classroom life (Parsons, 1958; Jackson, 1968; Dreeben, 1968), some instructional activities allow for public evaluation more than others. During recitation, for example, a child's social behavior and academic performances are constantly open to appraisal by both teacher and peers. During individualized projects, however, behavior and evaluations are usually private. Moreover, comparative assessments of pupils' task performances can only occur, *ipso facto,* when children are engaged in the same activity. The visibility or publicness and comparability of evaluation, then, differ by task.

Besides differences among certain tasks, the utilization of various activities may differ from classroom to classroom. Although most teachers apparently rely on recitation (Hoetker and Ahlbrand, 1969), some use very little of this activity. Classrooms themselves might be characterized by their distinctive utilization of instructional activities – by their task organization. Furthermore, just as research on the organization of work has shown that certain task characteristics affect patterns of interaction among work group members, the organization of classroom tasks may influence the types of social relationships that develop between teacher and pupils and among pupils. That is, task differences may account for other differences in a classroom's social organization.

Although many different aspects of interpersonal behavior in classrooms could be examined, several factors seem most salient. In examining teacher-pupil relationships the importance of sanctioning is readily apparent. One of the teacher's main functions is to control pupils' social behavior by rewarding appropriate acts and punishing misbehavior (Waller, 1932; Gordon, 1957; Bush, 1954; Kounin, 1970). Although teachers generally are limited in the kinds of sanctions they may employ (Dreeben, 1968), there are significant differences among teachers in the methods of control: Some rely on their ability to control certain organizational sanctions, such as grades; others tend to use their personal rapport with their pupils to exercise control (Waller, 1932). These different types of control indicate variations in the exercise of teacher authority. It has been noted that supervisory-subordinate relations in industrial work groups are affected by the organization of work (Woodward, 1958). In classrooms, to what extent are variations in the exercise of teacher authority linked to differences in classrooms' task structures? The organization of activities may influence the nature of teacher control and teacher-pupil relations.

Classroom control, however, is not just the exercise of teacher power; rather, it is the establishment of a definition of the situation that specifies the rules for appropriate behavior and performance within the classroom. This definition is negotiated by teacher and pupils jointly as they interact within the context of classroom activities. Hence teacher authority depends, in part, on the definition of appropriate behavior and sanctioning associated with particular classroom task structures.

Another major function of teaching involves providing appropriate instruction. An important part of a teacher's skill is the "ability to handle day-to-day fluctuations in the response to instruction by individual students and collectively by the classroom group" (Bidwell, 1965, p. 975). The teacher must be able to identify pupils' problems and provide the assistance necessary to help them benefit from instructional activities. However, the organization of task activities may affect the teacher's ability to treat particular problems effectively. By specifying the size of the work group and the number of different tasks occurring simultaneously in the classroom, the task structure may limit or enhance the teacher's opportunity to provide special assistance to individual pupils. For example, group activities involving the entire class may preclude the teacher providing needed immediate special assistance. How do teachers who use large group activities allocate assistance during that activity and at other times? More generally, what is the relationship between assistance patterns and task structure in a classroom?

In addition to teacher-pupil relationships, we shall explore two aspects of peer relations. First, just as in industrial work settings, the organization of tasks may influence the sociometric structure of a classroom. To what extent will the activity organization influence a child's choice of work and play associates? Patterns of association, however, are not the only important aspects of peer interaction; the quality of peer relations must be considered. We shall also examine the degree of cooperation and competition among children because it has important consequences for classroom social structure, particularly to the extent that a teacher can rely on friendly sharing and helping behavior among pupils. How does a classroom's task organization and evaluation system influence cooperative and competitive behavior among pupils? The nature of task activities and the evaluation of performance may affect interpersonal evaluations and the development of status systems within classrooms.

To summarize, then, the structure of task activities – a classroom's organization of instruction – creates the context in which teacher and pupils interact and social relationships form. Classroom tasks, like industrial work tasks, may differ in the basic elements of their work organization, such as in the size of the work group, the number of different tasks being worked on at the same time (the division of labor), the extent of pupil choice or teacher dominance over the task activities, and the type and degree of interdependence of performance evaluations. Classrooms that differ in their utilization of various task activities also may develop different patterns of social relationships: Variations in the exercise of teacher authority, in the allocation of instructional assistance, and in the structure of peer networks may be associated with differences among classroom task organizations. The research that follows, then, describes how classroom task activities differ in their organization of work, the impact of task organization on patterns of interaction within classrooms, and why particular social relationships develop in classrooms characterized by certain distinctive task organizations. It extends the activity structures perspective into the school and identifies important mechanisms affecting pupils and teachers.

2. The setting and study design

To explore possible relationships between classroom activity structures and emerging social relations, a research design was necessary that allowed for the generation of analytic categories and for the testing of preliminary notions. Initially, two third-grade rooms in a university-operated private school, Harper School,[1] were selected for observations. The principal of the school was advised about the topic of the research and asked to describe the teaching methods of his third-grade teachers. Because of the hypothesized relationship between classroom task activities and social relationships, the two classrooms selected were known to have teachers who taught "differently." No attempt was made to select classrooms according to pupil composition or other aspects of teacher background. The assignment of pupils to classrooms in this school balanced groups in terms of achievement levels and behavioral characteristics: Each classroom contained approximately equal numbers of high and low achievers and behavior problems. Most of the children in the school, though, can read at least at grade level, have I.Q.'s in the range of 110 to 145, and come from upper-middle-class families.

Each of these two third-grade classrooms was observed three to four hours per week for six months. Observation periods ranged from forty to sixty minutes and were scheduled in a rotating sequence to sample all activities in which the classes normally engaged – homeroom activities plus special classes in art, gym, science, and foreign language. During these periods, field notes were taken to provide as accurate a record of classroom events and interactions as possible. No coding or preset categories were used during these observations. Informal conversations with the teachers, pupils, the principal, and counselors also occurred whenever possible, and notes on these conversations were recorded immediately following the interactions.

During this exploratory part of the study, a preliminary categorization of classroom task activities was developed (see Chapter 3). Also, several differences in patterns of interaction between teacher and pupils and among the pupils were first noted. For example, peer associations in one classroom seemed to change frequently, while friendship groupings remained very stable in the other classroom. Moreover, friendship pairings seemed to match only children who were performing at the same level on classroom assignments in the stable grouping, while academic performance seemed to have little influence on friendship choice in the other classroom. In order to discover whether this difference and others were a consequence of the particular teachers and children studied or a result of differences in the task organization of the classrooms, several other classrooms were added to the study.

At the beginning of the next school year, two fourth-grade classrooms were included. With the cooperation of the school's principal, children were assigned to fourth-grade classrooms so that each class contained approximately half of the pupils from each of the third-grade classrooms. The assignment of pupils to these classrooms was not random. The third-grade teachers had grouped their children into pairs or triplets reflecting friendship ties during that year, and made recommendations to separate children who "did not get along well together." In addition, several children left the school, and one parent requested the assignment of her daughter to a particular fourth-grade teacher. Within these restrictions, the principal assigned the children to the fourth-grade classrooms in order to balance the groups in terms of achievement levels and behavior problems. However, the fourth-grade assignments seemed to mix the children from the two third-grade classrooms adequately. Some friendship groupings were retained, others split; all achievement levels were represented; each class had an equal number of identified behavior problems; and each of the third-grade classrooms was represented. Furthermore, the teaching methods of the selected fourth-grade teachers were known to differ in ways similar to the two third-grade teachers. Aside from teaching method differences, other background characteristics of these teachers were similar. All four had at least several years teaching experience at their grade level in this school. Table 2.1 presents the composition of the fourth-grade classrooms.

The assignment of half the pupils from each third-grade classroom to a teacher who "taught the same or differently" from their previous year's teacher allowed for the observation of how children with similar and different classroom experiences reacted in new classrooms. In other

Table 2.1. *Fourth-grade classroom pupil composition*

| | Fourth-grade class | | | |
	Field	Park	Other	Total
Third-grade class				
Hunt	9	7	9	25
Stone	9	10	5	24
Other	5	4	–	–
Total	23	21	–	–

words, would the children exhibit similar interaction patterns within classrooms having similar task organizations and different patterns within different task organizations? Or were the patterns observed in the third-grade classrooms attributable to the particular teachers and children? The third-grade teachers also were studied in order to observe how they would respond to a new group of pupils.[2] Would their use of tasks vary from the previous year? Would similar or different patterns of interaction develop? To address these questions, the design for the second part of this research consisted of a comparative case study of four classrooms with longitudinal data on thirty-five children and two teachers for two school years.

Before the beginning of the second school year, all four teachers were interviewed in order to learn about their curriculum plans, scheduling of activities, expectations about the new year and their new pupils, and their educational philosophy. This enabled the researcher to develop an observation plan and to compare subsequent classroom events and teacher comments with these early perceptions. The third-grade teachers also were asked to describe the academic strengths and weaknesses as well as the behavior problems of their former pupils.

All four classrooms were observed during the first hour of the new school year (with the assistance of three trained observers). Subsequently, classroom observations continued, with forty- to sixty-minute periods, three to four hours per classroom each week, scheduled in a rotating sequence to sample all activities in which the children participated (academic subjects, lunch, recess, and special classes). Each classroom was observed for twenty-one weeks. Again, field notes were recorded during observation periods to provide as accurate an account of activities and interactions as possible.

In addition to observations during classroom activities, informal conversations with teachers, pupils, the principal, counselors, and parents occurred frequently. Notes of these conversations were recorded as soon after the encounter as possible. Also, several formal interviews were scheduled. During the third, seventh, and twenty-first weeks of observations, the teachers were asked to describe the progress of their pupils and assess each child's academic and behavior problems. During the ninth and tenth weeks, all of the fourth-grade children were interviewed. Each was asked to compare his previous year's teacher with his current teacher, as well as to talk about his preferences concerning curriculum, classroom activities, and fellow pupils. (See Appendix A for the interview schedules.)

The data for this study, then, consist of three main items. First, the observation notes provide an accurate record of the activities and interactions that occurred within the classrooms. These notes describe the "natural history" of each classroom: what events and interactions occurred, when, and in what context. This record allows one to trace the development of events within each classroom and compare events among classrooms. Second, informal conversations with teachers, children, the principal, counselors, and parents provided information on these individuals' perceptions and expectations. In addition, these conversations often produced information about events for which the observer was not present. It was not uncommon for a teacher or child to approach the researcher to describe an event missed by the latter. Third, formal interviews with teacher and pupils provided specific and comparable responses to certain fixed questions and provided information on teachers' and pupils' perceptions of specific classroom events (e.g., why they thought no one wanted to play with Bobby). Notes detailing these conversations were recorded during or as soon after the encounter as possible. At the end of each day, notes from all three sources were typed onto ditto masters from which duplicate copies for analysis were obtained.[3]

Data analysis

The analysis of these sources of data followed what Glaser and Strauss (1967) have termed the "constant comparative method." That is, analysis occurs simultaneously with data gathering. As patterns and relationships are perceived in the data, they are investigated and new field plans are developed to illuminate relationships further or discover new patterns. This can be done following the three stages Becker (1958) has outlined for the "sequential analysis" of field data. First, indices are developed recurrently to test observed relationships in the field setting. Second, a frequency and distribution check is made of these indices to confirm or refute the existence of the hypothesized patterns. This check can be made on data already gathered by coding the field notes for the new indices or by coding subsequent field observations. Third, the researcher constructs a partial model of the social organization of the field setting, including those patterns confirmed by the frequency and distribution checks. As the research continues, new parts of the model are added and new observation plans and indices are developed. Illustrative of this process in this study was the investigation of the relationship between classroom task organization and peer competition. During the first part of this research, peer groupings seemed more stable and related to academic performance in one classroom than in the other. Using the task organization categories developed in the preliminary stage of research and sociometric plottings relating friendship, work, and play group membership among the children, the relationship between tasks and peer associations was explored and confirmed (see Chapter 5). The constant comparative method is particularly useful in the analysis of social processes because it allows the researcher to examine the social organization of a setting as it emerges. As events occur, they can be examined within the developmental context of the setting.

Intensive observation and informal interviewing overcome many of the methodological limitations of other, more common classroom research techniques. Recent observational research has relied largely on fixed category observation systems that focus on properties of dyadic interactions between the pupil and the teacher or among pupils (e.g., Flanders, 1960; Medley and Mitzel, 1963; Simon and Boyer, 1967; Brophy and Good, 1974). One major problem with most interaction rating schemes is that they ignore entire sets of social behavior that occur in classrooms (Bossert, 1975). In many cases only a small proportion of interaction occurs strictly with dyads: In lectures, for example, teachers often talk to the entire class. Even in those situations in which a teacher interacts directly with only one pupil, others may participate in and be influenced by that interaction. Classrooms are public places.

When a pupil is praised or punished, it is often in the presence of others; and this most certainly affects those observing as well as those interacting. By concentrating on the properties of dyadic relations, most classroom research has overlooked the social or group context of teacher and pupil behavior. Ethnographic techniques, however, allow for the detailing of complex interaction effects that occur within a learning setting. The dyadic unit can be placed within the context of broader social organizational features as social relationships develop. Moreover, by pairing ethnographic observation and informal interviewing, information can be collected on teachers' and pupils' perceptions of themselves and of others and, hence, on how their behavior is oriented during interaction. Social relationships, after all, are more than just the frequency of discrete types of behavior: They form as individuals take into account the meanings of others' actions (Weber, 1947; Mead, 1934). Fixed category scales, particularly those employing timed samples of behavior, assume that the number of occurrences of particular types of behavior adequately characterizes a social relationship, that statistically significant differences among frequencies of behavior constitute "real" differences in social relationships. Conceptually, this is unwarranted and, perhaps, accounts for the failure of these dyadic instruments to describe significant classroom differences. Although field research techniques usually do not provide data amenable to statistical manipulation, they do yield a rich and appropriate data base for sociological analysis.

The researcher's role in this school was not one of passive observer. Although responsibility for instruction and control of a classroom was never assumed, the observer frequently interacted with the children and teachers during observation periods. The children often asked for help on assignments, sought assistance in spelling a word, or simply wanted to talk. Occasionally, this was problematic because note taking was interrupted or severely limited during these interactions. However, the rapport established with the children seemed to stimulate their informant roles, therefore justifying the decreased accuracy of the classroom record. Because the school often has visitors and observers, most of the children seemed to accept the explanation that the observer was "interested in what third- and fourth-grade children do." The researcher also talked informally with teachers as often as possible.[4] Conversations occurred while the children were working, during recess, and during coffee breaks. These informal conversations created opportunities to question the children and teachers about specific events that had occurred, without arranging formal interviews.

In summary, this research followed an observational methodology using comparative case study and longitudinal designs. The data collected allow for the examination of the development of teacher-pupil and peer relationships within each classroom and for the comparative analysis of the influence of classroom task organization on these social relationships. Because activity types can be compared within each classroom as well as between classrooms representing different types, the observed differences are likely to reflect differences in the task organizations of the classrooms rather than particular teacher and pupil differences. Furthermore, because two groups of children were observed for two consecutive years, one with similar classroom task experiences and one with differing classroom task experiences, comparisons among the same children and between task organizations can be made.

It should be noted explicitly, however, that Harper School is not representative of American elementary schools in general. Its selective, private status, the dominant upper-middle-class student population, and the extraordinary amount of autonomy granted teachers temper the generality of this study's findings. But even though particular manifestations of social relations may vary with other factors, such as students' social class backgrounds and school organizational characteristics, the examination of these classrooms provides a good illustration of the relationships between task organization and forms of social relations.

3. Four classrooms

Classrooms are, for the most part, extremely similar. Not only do they have relatively uniform physical properties – blackboards, wastebaskets, bulletin boards, roll-down maps, desks, chairs, and tables – but they also provide fairly similar social contexts – there are teachers, pupils, curriculum segments in math, science, English, and social studies, and recess. It is somewhat misleading, however, to focus on these common properties of the school when analyzing schooling processes. Although classroom environments may appear similar and curriculum sections may have identical titles, activity structures and the patterns of interaction among class members vary substantially among classrooms. Particularly in an elementary school, where the school day is not segmented into separate subject areas taught by different teachers, the particular flow of events and activities in a classroom creates a distinctive context in which fairly stable and important social relationships emerge.

Before analyzing some of the sources of classroom differences, a sense of the commonalities and contrasts among the classrooms at Harper School must be given. Particular attention has been taken to provide accurate detail and events representative of the "everyday life" of the pupils and teachers without collapsing the richness and uniqueness of occurrences into analytic categories. These descriptions, then, serve as a data base for assessing the appropriateness of analytic categories and propositions that will follow.

Ms. Hunt's classroom (third grade)

On entering this classroom,[1] one usually finds Ms. Hunt at the front blackboard leading a recitation on social studies, math, or language. The children sit at their desks, some actively participating, others just listening. Hunt tries very hard to keep all her pupils interested in the activity; she usually calls on every pupil at least once during any recitation session. When a child does not pay attention, Hunt is quick to admonish the child to listen and participate.

Recitation is the most common activity; even the process of titling a paper took this form:

> [Monitors have passed out paper.]
>
> Hunt: (standing at front board) OK, now we have to put on a title for this exercise. Who can guess what it might be?
>
> (Hands raised)
>
> Amy.
>
> Amy: Spelling dictation number three.
>
> Hunt: (writing Amy's suggestion on the board) OK. Who agrees with Amy?
>
> (All raise their hands.)
>
> Good. Now, who can remember where this title goes?
>
> (Hands raised)
>
> Chris.
>
> Chris: Centered, below your name and date.
>
> Hunt: Good, now let's do that just as I have put it on the board.
> [As class writes the title, Ms. Hunt goes around the room checking to see if everyone has it correct.]
>
> Now, raise you hand if you are ready to go on.
>
> (All raise their hands.)
>
> [Note: this example was taken from the third week of school. However, similar events regularly occurred over titling the spelling dictation sheet as late as the sixth month of school.]

Everything from instructions to correcting homework could involve recitation. In fact, the daily "opening" also followed the recitation format. Each morning, after the children had put their coats and lunch boxes away, were seated at their desks, and the attendance had been taken, the class monitor led the flag salute. Hunt would then go to the front board and ask the class for the "date dictation," which involved three or four children spelling out the day, month, year, and complete date in numerical form (e.g., 9/27/73). After each dictation, Hunt asked the class to "verify" the dates by raising their hands if they agreed with the dictations given. Occasionally, a pupil would recite the date incorrectly; the dictation would be repeated until the class agreed it was correct.

Class votes on the correctness of fellow pupils' answers occurred quite frequently. Hunt felt that this process allowed the children to "have their say in the answer." It enabled her to check which children knew the answer and which did not. This public checking and voting, however, also allowed the children to see how well fellow pupils were doing. When a pupil did not raise his hand to vote, Hunt would ask why.

[Math recitation]

Hunt: How many agree with David that the answer is 12?

(All raise their hands, except Kelly.)

Kelly, what do you think?

Kelly: (She shrugs her shoulders as if she doesn't know.)

Hunt: Well, Kelly, what is 9 minus 7?

Kelly: Two.

Hunt: And, what is 7 minus 6?

Kelly: Uh, one.

Hunt: Then why weren't you sure that 79 minus 67 was 12?

Kelly: I don't know.

Hunt: Did you get it right on your paper?

Kelly: (shakes her head no)

However, sometimes children would vote with the majority even if they had a different answer.

[English recitation]

Hunt: OK, who has the answer to Part C?

(Raised hands)

OK, Karen.

Karen: (spells) *r-u-n-i-n-g*.

Hunt: How many agree with Karen?

(Most of the children raise their hands – some only raise their hands halfway.)

Well, what do you think?

(All raise their hands.)

Well, I don't think you're correct. Running is spelled *r-u-n-n-i-n-g*.

Remember the rule?

Susie: (shouting out) I had it correct.

Hunt: I really think everyone should go back and reread the rules again. Turn to page 36.

[Hunt goes on to read and explain the rules.]

(Susie turns to Pat: I had it right all the time!)

When this class was not doing recitation, the children usually worked on various work sheets and booklets. During this seat work activity,

Hunt often patrolled the classroom, assisting pupils and making sure everyone was working. Periodically, Hunt would conduct "conferences" with each pupil during these seat work periods in order to give individual attention and to help children with particular problems as well as to review their work. These conferences usually were held at the center table around which all the desks were lined. While conferences were being held, the rest of the class was supposed to work quietly on projects Hunt had listed on the board, in the order she specified. However, Hunt seemed to spend more time helping other pupils who came up to the table, quieting children who were "sharing too loudly," and checking to see which children had finished the various projects listed on the board than she did assisting the pupil with whom she was conferring.

> [Conferences at center table on spelling work. Class working individually at seats on math or social studies assignments.]
> (Ms. Hunt finishes with Chris and calls George to table.)

Hunt: Andrew, that is enough. (Talking to Martin.)

> (Hunt goes back to working with George. Lynn comes up to table and asks Ms. Hunt a question about her assignment.)
> (Hunt [spending about a minute] helps her. Carol comes up to ask a question.)

Hunt: Announcement. I want your attention. Who has done question five on this math?

Martin: What page?

Hunt: Page 106.

> (No one raises his hand.)

OK, when you get up to that one, ask Lynn about it because I gave her a hint on how to do it. Who is finished with their social studies? Karen (who has her hand raised), you can start on your math.

Martin, you too.

Get working. Now, we only have three minutes left so let's work hard.

> (Hunt sits down to work with George again. She notices Martin and Andrew playing swords with their pencils.)

Hunt: Martin and Andrew! Martin come over here.

> (Hunt gets up and brings Martin over to center table. She bawls out Martin – telling him that he should work harder. Lynn comes up to Hunt at center table and reminds her that it is time to go to gym. Hunt tells George that they will continue tomorrow and to go to his seat.)

Hunt: All right children, work away. Let's get ready to go to gym.

In addition to recitation and seat work, Hunt used some small group projects. Children occasionally worked in groups to complete a mural or poster, although, such projects occurred quite infrequently. One reason for this was that Hunt felt that the special art classes (about two hours per week) provided ample opportunity for the children to draw and paint. The only regular activity that split the class into smaller work groups was math. After several weeks of informal testing on math skills, Hunt felt that her class was too heterogeneous in ability to work as an entire group. In the seventh week of school, she divided the class into two math groups. Each group used the same book; however, one group started at Chapter 3, whereas the other began with Chapter 1. At first, Hunt worked with one group while the other one worked silently at their seats, but this method created considerable problems. Hunt was often interrupted by pupils from the group with which she was not working. They were either talking too loudly and needed control or wanted to ask a question. After several weeks, Hunt added an assistant teacher to help during math. Hunt worked with one group, while the assistant helped the other in the back room. Even though the class was divided into two smaller work groups, math always consisted of recitation or seat work.

Compared with the other three classrooms in this study, two aspects of Hunt's class are notable: the ritual adherence to the class schedule and the small amount of free time. Rarely did Hunt deviate from the class schedule she made at the beginning of the year. If an activity took more time than anticipated, it would either be postponed until the next day or rescheduled into one of two "flexible" periods included in the weekly schedule; and, aside from the twenty-minute morning recess period, the children in Hunt's class had little free time during the day. Recess was the only period in which the children could interact freely. Even during lunch, the children rarely had the opportunity to play together. Most of the thirty-minute lunch period was spent eating, and the children had to remain at their desks until they finished lunch.[2] The remaining time was often taken up by "announcements" made by either Hunt or the pupils.

[Lunch]

Hunt: (getting up from her desk and going to the front of the room) Announcement. Announcement. I'm going to count to five and see if everyone can be paying attention. One, two, three, four – Robert get in your seat and sit down while you're eating – five. Oh, I like the way Ellen is paying attention. OK. I need to know who wants to help with the pumpkin seeds we're going to roast.

(Lynn and Karen raise hands to volunteer.)

Good. That's all.

[Children go back to eating and talking – about two minutes elapse.]

(Martin goes up to Ms. Hunt and reminds her that he wanted to share a book he brought to school.)

Hunt: (going to the front) Oh, class, I forgot. Announcement. Martin has something to share. Kelly (talking to Jenny). Now, we must all remember to listen carefully when someone has something to share.

George, sit down (getting up to go to wastebasket).

OK, Martin.

[Martin takes about four minutes to share his book on state capitals. Hunt stands by him, reprimanding children who talk or try to get out of their seats.]

By the end of the eighth week of school, most of the children seemed to learn that it was best to remain in their own seats during lunch. When announcements used up the entire period, Hunt often promised that the class could play a game later in the afternoon. Usually, this consisted of a math game called "astronaut" in which two children tried to be the first to give the correct sum or product of an equation asked by Hunt, the winner challenging the next child. Although most of the children seemed to enjoy this game, it did not allow them to interact freely: It was a recitation.

Hunt seemed in constant control of the activities of her class. Very few things were done without her permission. Children could not talk without her permission; when the class began an assignment requiring a titled answer sheet, no one could copy the second word in the title until Hunt "verified" that the first word was correctly written on each paper; the children had to "sign out" in a special box marked on the blackboard to go to the bathroom; and everywhere the class went, it traveled in lines led by Hunt. Ms. Hunt made it very clear that she was in charge. In addition to telling the class her rules during the first hour of the year, she rigorously enforced her control. When a child talked out of turn or wrote the whole title on his paper before the first word was verified, Hunt sternly reminded her pupils of the classroom rules. This seemed effective because by the sixth week most pupils waited for their turn to talk and checked their work with Hunt before they began a new problem.

Hunt responded positively to pupils who constantly followed classroom rules. By the end of the third week, three girls who were the best behaved in the class began receiving much of Hunt's favor. They were often called on to help or run errands, and they were allowed to work together on their assignments in the back room while the rest of the class worked independently at their seats. Hunt said of them, "Janet, Erica, and Lynn are so well behaved. They're just a dream. I don't think I'll have any trouble with them the whole year." In addition to being the most well behaved, these three girls were also among the top performers in social studies, math, and language. Their work was often displayed to the class, and they received extra attention and help on their assignments.

[During seat work on maps]
Hunt: Put your things away. I want to take a little time to let Erica and Lynn present a little report they did on Ethiopia. While you all have been working on your map study skills, they have gone to the library and looked up a few things about Ethiopia [the country the class is going to study for social studies]. And, they've even made a few drawings to show you some of the things they've learned. Now pay attention. Girls.
[Erica and Lynn give their report and show several pictures.]

Besides using these three girls as academic examples for the class, Hunt also relied on two of the girls to serve as models for correct social behavior. In the thirteenth week of the school year, Hunt decided to separate two other girls who had been continually talking and misbehaving. She moved one of the girls by Lynn and moved Erica next to the other.

[Conversation with Ms. Hunt during recess]
Researcher: I noticed that Ellen and Jenny were moved apart.
Hunt: Oh yes. You've seen how they just talk and talk. I had to move them because they just didn't seem to respond to my talks with them. I moved Erica by Jenny and put Ellen into Erica's old seat [by Lynn]. I hope Lynn and Erica can be good examples for them. They [Lynn and Erica] are such good students. Ellen and Jenny won't have someone always to gossip with. I think Jenny will be OK, but Ellen is going to be a hard one to deal with. She's the initiator of a lot of the trouble.

Even though this manipulation seemed to eliminate some of Ellen's and Jenny's inappropriate behavior, the two pairs of new neighbors never really became friends. Ellen began talking with Susie, her other seat-mate, and a friendship developed. Jenny, whose only other seatmate was a boy, withdrew from peer relations. Erica and Lynn, however, continued to associate during work periods and often ate lunch together. Several weeks after Hunt had moved the girls, Erica and Lynn asked to be moved back together, and Hunt approved.

Generally, the seating arrangement was an important factor in peer associations. Because the children rarely had time to interact outside of task activities and because most task activities involved pupils working in their own seats, most peer interactions occurred among seatmates. Although the children were allowed to pick their own seats at the first of the year, all subsequent seating changes had to be approved by Hunt. Hunt also made several seating changes like the one involving Ellen, Jenny, Erica, and Lynn in order to separate misbehaving pupils. When these seating changes were made, they tended to affect friendship patterns. For example, George and Andrew gradually stopped associating after George was moved because of their continual talking. Ten days after the move, each began associating primarily with his new seatmate. Hunt's control over seating, then, seemed to have an important influence over peer relationships in this classroom.

Another aspect of classroom organization that influenced peer relations was math grouping. After the two math groups had been formed in the seventh week of school, several friendship pairs split when the children were placed in different groups. Karen and Anne, for example, had been friends for two years and always were together during the first weeks of the year. After they were placed in separate math groups, Anne began working with Ellen, who was in the same math group. When Anne began including Ellen in games with Karen, several "fights" occurred. Five weeks later, Anne and Ellen became "best friends," excluding Karen. Friendships, in general, tended to develop among children who sat next to each other and who also were achieving at similar levels in the classroom. This seemed to be reinforced by Hunt's tendency to pair pupils by their achievement level when the class worked in small groups.

[Ms. Hunt tells the children to work in pairs on the set of problems she passes out.]

(Karen gets up and goes over to ask Patty if she wants to work with her. Ms. Hunt sees this and goes over to Karen.)

Hunt: Now Karen, I think it would be better if you worked with Carol.

(Ms. Hunt takes Karen by the hand and has her sit by Carol.)

You girls can work best together. Patty and Laurie are not up to page 56 yet and they need some extra help.

[Karen and Carol are in group 1 – the top math group – while Patty and Laurie are in group 2. Ms. Hunt does not give Patty and Laurie any extra help that day.]

As controller of task activities, Hunt dominated events in her classroom and left few opportunities for her pupils to choose their own tasks or to interact freely with each other. However, Hunt exercised her control with warmth, skill, and equity. Her class proceeded from task to task in an orderly and disciplined manner. There were always things to do and the assistance available for doing them.

Mr. Stone's classroom (third grade)

It was often very difficult to find Mr. Stone and his pupils;[3] if their schedule indicated that they should be in their room doing math or language arts, instead they might be outside flying model airplanes to judge the relationship between time and distance, measuring a room or hallway to understand spatial perspective, taking a walking tour of the neighborhood, or just having a play break. As its title indicated, Stone's schedule was "tentative and vague." He often changed the daily plan in order to take advantage of a clear day or a special program. Stone, though, was not the only one to initiate changes. His pupils also suggested modifications in the schedule when they wanted to do something new. Class votes on such proposed changes were quite common.

[Stone had just finished reading a story.]

Stone: Well, we still have math left to do. Let's . . .

Anne: (interrupting) Let's play ball now and do math later.

(Several kids agree.)

Stone: Well, when are you going to do your reports?

Anne: Later.

Robert: I want to do mine today.

(Tim and John agree.)

Anne: But we can do those this afternoon.

Stone: When?

Anne: After foreign language.

Stone: OK, it's up to you guys. As long as math sheets and reports get done by Thursday. How many want to play ball?

(Fourteen)

OK, that's a majority. Go do it.

In addition to using schedule changes to take advantage of special events, Stone also kept his class schedule flexible in order to accommodate his pupils' changing interests.

[Math recitation]

Stone: [at side board] Now, who has got an answer to the next problem?

(Only Bill raises his hand.)

Anyone besides Bill have an answer today? What is this? You all were doing this yesterday. It's review. What's the answer Bill?

Bill: 346

Stone: Karen, can you check this?

Karen: (shakes her head no)

Stone: Anyone? (no response) Well, I think we'd might as well give this up for today. I don't know what's wrong.

(Stone walks back to his desk.)

Let's read until gym. Do it!

(Kids put math books away and begin reading.)

Stone used very little recitation in his classroom. Although recitation was used more frequently at the beginning of the year when he was trying to judge his pupils' capabilities, the amount of recitation steadily decreased after the first two weeks. The two most common tasks in this classroom were language arts work sheets and independent reading. Stone had a complete set of puzzles and work sheets from the Electric Company (television show) that served as the core of his language curriculum. Since the work sheets were not graded, the children worked together in completing them while Stone sat at his desk doing paper work or the work sheets themselves. If a child was having a problem, Stone gave helpful hints or encouragement; however, he rarely patrolled the room checking each child's progress.

Each week several class periods were devoted to reading, and every child was expected to have and be reading a book. Periodically, Stone conducted individual reading sessions with each pupil in which the child read aloud from his current book. He tried to have his pupils read more challenging books as their reading improved and allowed them to visit the library nearly as often as they pleased. Stone also liked to read aloud to the class. When he did read, the children were free to draw, read, work on assignments, or just listen as long as their activity did not disturb those listening.

In addition to work sheets and reading, Stone used a number of "projects" in his curriculum. One of the favorite projects was pantomime. The children divided themselves into small groups, planned the scene they wanted to perform, and practiced. After a while, the whole class gathered and each group performed its skit. Usually the children acted out a nursery rhyme scene or Mother Goose story, like "Little Red Riding Hood" or "Goldilocks and the Three Bears." Occasionally, Stone would duplicate some scripts from a children's play and the groups performed these. However, pantomime was the favorite. Other projects included plane flying, group reports, several math games, and writing a newspaper-magazine. Also, the children could learn to whittle, make yarn pictures and dolls, and macrame during numerous arts and crafts periods. Stone often brought in helpers to show the children how to begin; but once initial instructions were given, he usually let the children figure things out for themselves.

[Stone writing at his desk. About half of the class out of the room, collecting stories for the newspaper. The "editors" are meeting in the back room trying to decide what to include in their paper.]

(Anne comes out of the back room, up to Stone.)

Anne: Mr. Stone, they won't get anything done. David keeps goofing off.

Stone: That's not my problem. You're the editors.

Anne: But, we can't figure out what to have. David keeps saying he wants jokes and . . .

Stone: Anne, go back in there and do it yourselves; the editors have to make the decisions, not me.

(Anne goes into back room.)

[Ten minutes and three protests for help later, the editors had decided on a format and article list.]

Playtime was another important activity. Nearly four times as much time was allocated to play in Stone's as in Hunt's classroom. In addition to the thirty-minute or longer morning recess, Stone's class often played baseball in the afternoon. Most of the lunch period was occupied by play activities, and Stone rarely stopped lunchtime games to handle class business.

One exception to this general pattern occurred during the fourteenth through the eighteenth weeks of the school year when Ms. Kay, a student teacher, began conducting spelling and handwriting lessons as part of her training. While Kay had been in Stone's class since the fifth week, she only observed and occasionally helped children do their work sheets or math assignments. She had not instructed the entire class, nor had she engaged in any extensive disciplinary action. However, when conducting her own lessons, Kay primarily used recitation, and this contrasted sharply with Stone's use of instructional activities.

One of the biggest problems Kay faced was getting the children "settled down" to do her recitations. This was particularly hard to accomplish after Stone had been working with the class on a small group project.

> [Class working on crafts. Stone says time is up and that Ms. Kay is going to do handwriting. Children slowly clean up.]
>
> Stone: OK, let's get going. Ms. Kay wants to do the handwriting. In your seats!
>
> (Kay goes to the front board. Stone goes to desk.)
>
> Kay: I want everyone's attention. Billy stop that (shooting rubber bands into his desk). OK, let's get ready for our handwriting. John get your book out. Karen and Carol stop talking.
>
> (Class doesn't seem ready to quiet down.)
>
> Let's look up here. Robert, get your handwriting out – put your whittling away. Scott you too. Now today we're going to start on the second family. The letters . . .
>
> Karen that's enough (talking to Carol)!
>
> The letters are . . . Now class, are we going to do this or not (several talkers)?

During these transition periods, Kay had to spend much of the time gaining pupils' attention. It often seemed that the children were not accustomed to waiting for the teacher to organize the activity: They wanted to start on their own.

Because Stone used very little recitation, he did not spend much time in front of the entire class leading the activity. After he gave instructions, he expected the children to organize and complete their own tasks. From the beginning of the year, Stone made it clear that each pupil was responsible for his own work and time, and that he was not there to tell the class what to do but to supply help when needed.

> [Kids working on work sheet – in pairs or alone]

(Paul comes up to Stone's desk to ask a question.)

[He is the sixth one to ask the same question.]

Stone: I'm not going to answer any more of your questions. You all heard the instructions. I can't do it for you. Try it. Everyone of you can figure this one out.

In part, the use of work sheets and small group projects decreased the children's reliance on Stone. Stone could not help every group at the same time; hence most of the children learned to work out their own solutions.

[Stone having a reading conference with one pupil]

(Richard and Alan come up to Stone's desk – stand there waiting to be recognized. Stone finally does notice them.)

Stone: What do you guys want?

Alan: We can't figure out how to chart our results [from plane flying].

Stone: I can't help you now. I'm reading with Martha. You can figure it out for yourselves. Remember what I told you.

(Richard and Alan go back to desks and work.)

[Later in the period, the boys finally figure it out and proudly show Mr. Stone their chart.]

Stone refused to be the sole authority and director of action within the classroom. He did not always provide the correct answer or tell his pupils exactly what to do.

Moreover, Stone often participated with his pupils while they were working on a project. Not only did he do the Electric Company work sheets, whittle, make sketches of a room, and wind yarn for craftwork, but he also participated with his class during their special art, science, and gym classes. As a participant, Stone occasionally abdicated some of his leadership responsibilities. His pupils were often allowed to organize and run classroom projects, and Stone was "outvoted" several times when the class wanted to do a particular activity.

In addition to allowing the children many opportunities to choose their activities, Stone tried not to show any favoritism. When he had to assign tasks or group the class for projects, he usually assigned positions and groups by lottery, drawing buttons with pupils' names from a box. If Stone had favorite pupils, it was not evident in his classroom behavior. Although he tended to call on one boy for answers to the hardest questions during math recitation, Stone seemed to allocate his attention quite equally among pupils in his classroom. The pupils who did receive the most assistance were the ones who were having trouble with a project or in reading.

Most of the pupils in Stone's classroom seemed to respond to this atmosphere of choice by organizing their own activities. They did not wait for Stone to tell them to do something: They began work on their own. In contrast to Ms. Hunt's "opening ceremonies," as Mr. Stone's pupils arrived at school, they put their coats away, greeted their friends, and began reading, finishing a work sheet, or doing some other project. As the official starting hour approached, Stone surveyed the class, asked who was in the back room painting, and filled in the roll sheet. If he wanted to begin with a class activity, like math recitation, or make an announcement about a special event, he called the class to their seats; otherwise, there would be no formal commencement of the workday.

Another difference between Mr. Stone's and Ms. Hunt's classrooms was the extent of peer interaction. As mentioned earlier, peer relations in Hunt's class occurred primarily between seatmates and among members of the same math group. Because recitation and seat work activities dominated that classroom, there were few opportunities for the children to interact freely. However, in Stone's classroom, where the children were primarily involved in small group projects, peer associations were frequent and constantly shifting. Not only did the children choose their own seats, but they also changed seats when they wanted. Friendship groups seemed to change as often as new interests were begun. If an activity occurred that was of different interest to a friendship pair, each participated in separate tasks.

> [Class finishes math and Stone says to begin crafts work.]
> (Kids put away math books and get out their crafts. Ann and Karen [who finished some macrame during the last crafts period] go up to Mr. Stone and ask what they can do.)
> Stone: Well, there's whittling, the mural, your dolls. Or, you can do some more macrame. It's up to you.
> (Anne and Karen walk back to their desks, talking. Karen says she wants to whittle. Anne says she doesn't because you can get cut. They decide to do different crafts. Anne goes to help on mural and Karen begins whittling.)
> [Anne and Karen are best friends.]

This kind of exchange did not occur in Hunt's classroom. When free time or group projects were allowed, friendship groups usually remained together.

Stone's class might best be characterized as "very active." It often seemed that too many things were going on at once for him to direct all the action.

Ms. Field's classroom (fourth grade)

In many ways, Ms. Field's classroom resembled Ms. Hunt's; the similarity was greatest in the types of activities and patterns of interaction characterizing both classrooms. Like Hunt, Field used recitation as the basic instructional activity. Each morning, after roll was taken and homework collected, Field led the recitation in English, and then in math. In the afternoon, social studies usually followed a recitation format. When the children were not engaged in recitation, they were either reading from textbooks or completing a class or homework assignment.

Most tasks in Field's room were assigned to the entire class. Everyone had to read the same chapters, answer the same questions, or write a short story. The only regular individualized project was an independent reading laboratory (SRA) in which the children progressed at their own pace through a series of increasingly difficult exercises. Occasionally, Field used small group projects or allowed the children to choose what they wanted to do. Although these elective activities were more frequent than in Hunt's classroom, recitation and class assignments were the most prevalent instructional activities.

From the first day, Field exercised very tight control over her class. As the children first entered her room, Field greeted each one and told them that they had been assigned a number (alphabetically). The children were to locate the seat with their number on it and figure out the pattern in which Field had arranged the seats.

[From conversation]

Field: I use the seating pattern every year. It's a good way to start off with math – to make it fun. It usually takes two, maybe three days, for the children to get the pattern. We discuss it in math. Also, I can get a good idea of the behavior problems before I have them changing seats. I'm going to ask them to write down their choices and then I'll make the assignments.

She was the only teacher of the four studied in this book who assigned seats. Classroom rules were the first topic on the new year's agenda. Field thoroughly explained what tasks her pupils would be expected to do and how they were to be judged.

[Field up at front board, talking to the class]

Field: I'm not going to grade you now but I want you to know what I'm going to do. I'm putting everyone's name in a book – this one (she shows the book) and it has columns where I'm going to record what you do. One thing you have to learn is to make commitments and when you do not fulfill a commitment you get an X in the book . . . Also, you will get a folder later. You are to keep all your work in it to see what commitments you have met and how you are doing. Everything you do goes into the folder.

Field made it clear that performance was a very important part of life in her room. Not only did she begin assigning and grading homework from the first day, she also granted special privileges to those pupils who excelled in their work. During the second week, for example, four boys who had shown strong math abilities in their homework and in math recitation were dubbed the "math honor guard" by Field. These boys helped during demonstrations and generally monopolized math recitation.

[Math recitation]

(Field seems to call on the honor guard boys for the hardest problems and she often says these are the hardest ones.)

Carl [a math honor guard boy] is getting quite noisy, waving his hand and yelling "me" when Field asks a question.)

Field: (to Carl) Be patient, you'll get your turn later. I'm going to give you the most difficult question.

[Later]

Field: Now Carl, it's your turn. Come up to the board and explain problem 13.

[He does, correctly.]

Field: OK, since you boys [talking to the math honor guard – who all sit in the same row] have done so well, while I'm working with everyone, you go ahead and try to figure out problem 14. It's a hard one. Go in the back room and work together on it.

[Recitation continues and boys go into back room.]

Later, another group of pupils, those who consistently completed their homework assignments on time, was allowed to form a "castle committee" that designed and built a cardboard castle for its stuffed animals while the rest of the class worked on unfinished assignments.

The top performers in the class (the math honor guard, castle committee, and two other boys) received quite a bit of special attention from Field. She gave them extra assistance on their regular assignments and allowed them to work together on regular and special projects.

[Don walking in the hallway]

Researcher: Where are you going, Don?

Don: Library. Carl and I have a special project to do.

Researcher: What is it?

Don: Oh, we're supposed to look up some stuff about bases [math]. Ms. Field said we know multiplication well enough so we didn't have to stay while they reviewed. Carl wanted to do the report.

Often the top pupils were allowed to go to the library or into the back room to work while Field continued a recitation with the rest of the class.

Whereas the children from Ms. Hunt's classroom seemed to have little difficulty adjusting to Ms. Field's room, several of Mr. Stone's children had to learn that they had little say concerning classroom events.

[Field reading a story to the class]

(John is reading his own book – hiding it behind his desk – as Field reads.)

(Field sees John reading.)

Field: John bring that here. (She takes the book when he comes up.) It's mine now – no reading when I'm reading.

(John sits down again – as he passes the researcher he mutters: Mr. Stone let us read last year.)

[Field at front of room talking.]

Field: We're going to have a period of math and then we can go outside if everything gets done.

Class: AH!

David: Let's go out now and then do math.

Field: Watch your manners! No talking out. We'll do math now.

Karen: Let's vote on it.

Field: There will be no voting in my class!

Karen: In Mr. Stone's, we did.

Field: I don't care what happened last year. I make the decisions here!

Field was very firm in her control over pupils. She felt that the children needed to respect her authority or else activities could not run smoothly.

[Conversation]

Field: I'm really having trouble with some of Mr. Stone's kids. They are much less able to work together. Much less self-control. After all, they haven't learned that if they want to do something that they can't just do it anytime they please. You have to set limits for them . . . They just haven't learned to control themselves within an environment. Stone's kids have to learn to obey the rules of the society [meaning classroom]. They must learn to follow the rules. They need to know what authority is, or else we won't get anything done this year.

Just as the top performers were rewarded for their achievements, well-behaved pupils also were granted special privileges. The castle committee, for example, expanded to admit several children who were exceptionally well behaved, even though they had not finished all of their homework for the week. Also, several "rowdy" boys were excluded despite their perfect homework completion record. Field used these special privileges to control her children. She usually led recitations from the front of the room and always demanded that children raise their hands and wait their turn to answer. When the children worked at their seats, she patrolled the classroom, checking each pupil's progress and making sure no one was talking or playing. Although she did not march her class in lines from their room to special classes, she did make her pupils line up and be silent before she dismissed them. Pupils also had to sign out to leave the classroom even if it was just to go to their lockers in the hallway. As one child put it, "Ms. Field, she's not soft. You can't goof around like you could sometimes in Mr. Stone's room. Work is work, and if you don't do it, you know what will happen . . . she's the boss."

Peer relations in Ms. Field's classroom were similar to the pattern noted in Ms. Hunt's. Because recitation and individual seat work were the most frequent task activities, the children generally associated with their seatmates. During the third week, when last year's friendships began to weaken and new ones formed, the boys in the math honor guard began working and playing together during lunch and free time. In the fourth week, they asked Field if they could move their desks together in the back of the room. She approved, and the boys formed an entire row of top-achieving pupils who dominated math recitation and several other subjects. Later, the two top performers on SRA and three girls from the castle committee also moved together and began associating during free time. Field allowed these groups of children to work together on assignments and other projects while the rest of the class was working independently or with Field. As the school year progressed, this classroom became segregated according to levels of achievement. The top-performing pupils were the first to begin associating and working together. Later, the average pupils began excluding the poorest-performing pupils from their play and work groups, leaving these pupils either to form their own groups or play alone. For example, Alice and Karen were best friends in the third grade and always ate and played together at the beginning of the year. Although Alice was not a top pupil, she always got her homework in on time and joined the castle committee. Karen, however, had a very difficult time with math and rarely finished her homework. During several free-time periods, Alice worked with the castle committee, while Karen either played alone or worked on her assignments. After several weeks, Alice began spending more time with her new friends from the committee than with Karen. When Karen tried to join an ongoing game after she had finished her work, she was told she could not play. Soon, Karen just played alone or joined Robert and Terry, who also had to spend part of their free time finishing their assignments.

In many ways, these friendship patterns reflected a structure of competition that permeated this classroom. The children were aware of their own as well as their peers' performances. Field often commented publicly on each pupil's performance as she passed back tests or homework assignments. SRA and work folders were open for anyone to examine.

> [Class working at own seats on assignments]
> (David came up to SRA boxes – by researcher – and searches through for his booklet. He comments on each of the other pupils' color level.)
> David: (to researcher) You know, I got to skip red.
> Researcher: Yeah?
> David: Yep, now I'm second in the class. Only Carl is ahead. He skipped to green. But look at Josh (pulling out his booklet), he's still on tan. (laughs) I'm going to be through red in no time.

Furthermore, because special privileges in the class, like being in the castle committee and working together on projects and assignments, depended on a child's performance, competition became important. As one father noted, "There seems to be tremendous anxiety about remaining on the castle committee. David has mentioned it several times at the dinner table." However, rather than competing against the entire class, some of the children formed work and play groups that provided help on homework and class assignments.

Performance, then, was not only important for Field's treatment of her pupils but also for the peer relationships that developed in her classroom.

Ms. Park's classroom (fourth grade)

From the first day of class, Ms. Park allowed her children to choose many of the activities they wanted to do. The class did not merely vote on several alternatives Park had chosen; rather, the children were free to work individually or in small groups at a number of projects that both they and Park organized.

> [Park passed out spelling books and explained how they were
> to be used – first day of class.]

> Park: Now, you can either look at your spellers – I would like you
> to do the first exercise by Wednesday – or, you can look at the
> maps I have on the wall. They're on Greece and that's what we'll
> be studying in Social Studies. So – get yourself acquainted with the
> room.

> Kim: (raising her hand) Should we do our spelling now?

> Park: That's up to you.

It was not unusual to find Park's children scattered throughout her large room, in the halls, and at the library working alone or in pairs on a variety of projects. Although Ms. Park and Ms. Anthony (Anthony taught math while Park taught English to Anthony's class) used some recitation, small group and individual projects, reading, storywriting, and artwork were the most common tasks.

During the period this class was observed, the children and Park became involved in several extensive projects. For example, in the third week, the class decided (at Park's suggestion) to paint several large murals for the walls at a local children's hospital. For several weeks work on the mural progressed under the direction of Terry, the most talented artist in the class. Park played little part in designing and painting the mural. Terry was the one who organized the pictures, assigned tasks, and generally supervised the painting. Park did not officially appoint Terry as the mural organizer; Terry's leadership emerged because she was the one most capable of helping others with their sketching and painting and had the best ideas. When the children had free time or had finished an assignment, they checked with Terry to see what needed to be done and began work on the mural. Other projects included the writing and staging of a play, running a flea market to raise money for needy families at Christmas, and building models of volcanoes, mountains, and castles. Although Park often helped start or supervised some of these projects, the children themselves were usually in charge.

In addition to these projects the children had language, spelling, and math books from which to work. Park also expected that each child would be reading a book; like Mr. Stone, Ms. Park considered independent reading very important.

One very striking part of Park's class was the amount of free time. Besides gym and lunch period, Park always had a fifteen- to twenty-minute break in the morning and usually allowed a short play period in the afternoon. She seemed well aware that her children could only work so long without becoming bored or restless.

> [The children had been working for forty minutes on the stories they were writing.]
> Park: I think you've been working very hard and need a break. Those who need to go to the bathroom can.
> (Several kids go out to the bathroom. Terry comes over to Laurie and Ellen to talk about the Nancy Drew Club. Donald and Charles go to their chess game. The rest talk.)
> [Break lasts eighteen minutes.]

These breaks allowed the children to interact freely, as Ms. Park often left the room to have a short coffee break with Ms. Anthony.

> [Conversation]
> Park: The kids need some time of their own. I try to give them a break every so often so they can get a drink, stretch and go to the bathroom. It seems to defuse them. After a break they're usually ready to begin working again. Anyway, I have to have a cup of coffee and a cigarette, too.

This freedom of interaction seemed to stimulate a much more fluid peer network than in the other classrooms. Park's children were the first to make new friends among children who were not their classmates the year before. By only the third day of school, several children asked to have their seats changed in order to sit next to a new friend. Throughout the year, this group of children constantly changed seating arrangements; as new interests were formed, new friendship and work groups shifted.

[Conversation]

Park: Did you notice Donald and Jim?

Researcher: They were playing today.

Park: Yes, that is the first time Jim has really got involved with another child. He is so adult oriented. Ms. Anthony actually got them together on those math games. They were the only ones who could get the answer. And, they've made up several more puzzles together. Jim even moved his seat over by Donald.

In part, this changeability of peer relations seemed due to the fact that special projects and the considerable amount of free time provided the children with the opportunity to interact with a large proportion of their peers. One of the best examples of this was the formation of the Nancy Drew Mystery Book Club. At first, two girls, Laurie and Ellen, brought some of their Nancy Drew books to read during independent reading. May, who sat next to them, asked if she could borrow one of the books, adding that all three could trade and borrow each others' books so that they might compile a complete set to read. The girls thought that was a good idea, and with Park's permission they brought all of their books to school. Terry also became interested and brought in a few volumes the other three girls did not have. Soon all the girls in the class wanted to read the Nancy Drew books. Laurie and Ellen suggested starting a club, and eight girls began trading, reading, and talking about Nancy Drew during their free time and lunch hour. However, as interest waned and a fight occurred over ownership of several books, the club dissolved into several new friendship cliques, with Laurie and Ellen dropping their previously close friendship ties. Other groups formed, dissolved, and re-formed in response to interests such as chess, scrabble, math puzzles, war games, and playing jacks.

In contrast to Ms. Field's and Ms. Hunt's classrooms, there seemed to be very little evidence that academic competition or status influenced the formation of peer relations in Ms. Park's class. Although several girls expressed some envy of Terry's art ability, none of the friendship groups resembled the math honor guard or castle committee in Field's class. Many of the friendship groups that developed during the year contained children who were very different in their academic abilities. It seemed that game or project interest was more important than academic performance. For example, Donald, the class chess buff, took on any challengers and never refused to help classmates improve their game. Occasionally, some competition emerged during spelling tests and over who progressed faster through the language booklet. However, this competition rarely seemed to influence choices of friends or play groups.

Park seemed to rely on the cooperative atmosphere among her pupils in order to allow a large number of different tasks and projects to occur at the same time.

[Conversation]

Park: My kids have to be able to work together. Things really don't go well otherwise. I can't police one group while I'm working with another. It's good that I have several helpers this year. Terry is so good. She doesn't boss the kids and can really help on some things. Though, it was funny the other day – you weren't here – to see Ted helping Charles with his math. Talk about the blind leading the blind.

During periods when the children were involved in different projects, Park usually worked with pupils having difficulty with some task or assignment. Often she asked a child to help one or two pupils while she worked with others.

[Park finishes reading to class.]

Park: OK. Let's see what we can take care of for the rest of the afternoon. Let me see. Alice and Tracy, you need help on your spelling.

Tracy: We're almost finished with lesson 5.

Park: Good. Terry could you help them?

Terry: (nods her head yes)

Park: OK, go out into the hall. I want Ted, John, and Laurie to come with me and work on your handwriting. Bring your pencils and paper. Up here (pointing to front desks). And, the rest of you can read or . . .

[Class begins work.]

Most of Park's time was spent helping pupils find materials for their projects, suggesting new projects, and assisting pupils with difficult tasks.

Having the children involved in many different activities during the same period did create some problems. Park often could not keep track of everything each child was doing.

[Conversation]

Park: I had to fill out the grade sheets last week. Oh, was it hard. I kept thinking, now what did so-and-so do. Sometimes there is just too much going on to know. One week someone is having a problem and the next they're OK. Like Ted with his handwriting. What am I supposed to give him on handwriting?

Researcher: It seems really hard to know when you have a lot of different projects going on at the same time.

Park: Right. I only tend to see the end project or the struggle to get there. I used to have a lot of work sheets. Then, I knew how to evaluate each child. But it wasn't as much fun.

The classroom task structure

In terms of their organization of work, three distinctive patterns of classroom task organization emerge from the observation of these classrooms. *Recitation,* the most common instructional activity in both Ms. Hunt's and Ms. Field's rooms, is an activity that involves the whole class or a large group of children in a single task: The children listen to the question the teacher asks, raise their hands, wait to be recognized, and give an answer. Occasionally, children can ask questions when they do not understand the question or the materials, though the teacher usually controls the flow of questions and answers. During recitation, a child's performance is very public. Both the teacher and fellow pupils know when an answer is correct or incorrect. When the response is correct, the teacher usually praises the child, and when the response is incorrect, the teacher either corrects it or asks the same question of another pupil. Because of this, class members have a fairly good idea of how others are performing. Because the task and curriculum are the same for every pupil, performance can be easily compared.

Another task activity might be called *class task.* Work sheets, tests, math assignments, or other tasks assigned to the entire class fit into this category. In Mr. Stone's and Ms. Park's classrooms, the children organized some of their own class tasks; usually, however, the teacher assigns a common task for every pupil to complete. Performance on class task activities is less public than in recitation. Because the tasks are done independently or in small groups, neither all class members nor the teacher can constantly observe each other while they are working, though pupils' performances are comparable due to the common task.

The third type of task structure is the *multitask* organization, which usually includes tasks like independent reading, small group and independent projects, artwork, and crafts. These activities involve the greatest amount of pupil choice in organizing and completing the work. Like class tasks, multitask activities involve independent or small group work. The distinctive characteristic of multitask settings, however, is that many different tasks are being worked on simultaneously. Because the class is involved in a variety of task activities, the teacher and children are rarely able to observe the task performance of every pupil. Furthermore, pupils' performances cannot be compared except among those children doing the same task.

The structure of task activities, then, can be described in terms of the size of work groupings, the number of different tasks being completed at the same time (the division of labor), the amount of pupil choice in organizing the tasks, and the extent to which evaluations of task performance are public and comparable. Table 3.1 summarizes these characteristics for the three types of task organizations.

The frequency of these three task organizations varied substantially among the classrooms studied. Both Ms. Hunt and Ms. Field used a considerable proportion of recitation and seldom had multitask activities. Mr. Stone and Ms. Park relied largely on multitask and class task activities and used very little recitation. Table 3.2 presents the distribution of activities in the four classrooms.

Ms. Hunt's and Ms. Field's classrooms were recitation dominated, with nearly half the average school day spent doing this activity. Mr. Stone's classroom was characterized mostly by class task activities. Ms. Park's was a multitask organized classroom. Classrooms themselves, therefore, can be characterized in terms of their predominant task organization.

From the descriptions of the four classrooms, it should be noted that different social relationships developed in classrooms having

Table 3.1. *Work organization characteristics of classroom task organizations*

	Group size	Division of labor	Pupil choice	Evaluation
Recitation	Large group	Single task	Teacher control	Public; comparable
Class task	Individuals or small groups	Single task	Teacher control but some pupil choice	Less public; comparable
Multitask	Individuals	Many tasks	Extensive pupil choice	Less public; noncomparable

Table 3.2. *Classroom usage of task types – by percent of total class time*

	Recitation	Class task	Multitask	Free time	O[a]	Total	Hours
Hunt	49.4	27.3	9.6	3.6	10.1	100	41
Stone	19.3	36.3	25.6	11.8	7.0	100	46
Field	44.1	24.7	13.5	7.1	10.6	100	47
Park	20.3	22.9	33.5	17.2	6.1	100	50

Note: Observations made in Mr. Stone's and Ms. Hunt's classrooms during the first year of observations are not included in this table. However, the percentage figures presented are nearly identical to those recorded during that period.
[a]O represents the time spent on paper work and administration in the classroom (i.e., taking the roll, collecting milk money, passing out forms, etc.).

different task organizations. Considerable variation in the exercise of teacher authority, the allocation of individual instructional assistance, the formation of friendship groups, and the extent of cooperation and competition among children was observed. Ms. Hunt's and Ms. Field's classrooms operated under fairly strict teacher control. These teachers relied on their institutional role *qua* teacher to supervise pupils, and they tended to provide considerable special treatment to the pupils they identified as top performers. Peer relations in these two classrooms seemed to be influenced significantly by the structure of instructional tasks: Children were very competitive and chose friends within their own achievement subgroupings. By contrast, Mr. Stone and Ms. Park allowed their pupils considerable choice over classroom events. Their control relied less on their role as formal leader than on their personal rapport with the children. Pupil behavior problems generally were handled in private rather than in front of the entire class as in Ms. Hunt's and Ms. Field's classrooms. Pupil friendship groups changed frequently, and each included children achieving at different levels. These differences in social relationships among the classrooms at Harper School seem more a product of distinctive task organizations than individual characteristics of the teachers and pupils. The following chapters will explore these relationships.

4. The teacher-pupil relationship

In studying classroom differences, teacher control and the allocation of instructional assistance are two important features of teacher-pupil relationships. Among the four teachers observed in this study, there were considerable differences in the use of control sanctions, in the frequency with which these sanctions were employed, and in the amount of help given to particular children in the class. The two teachers who used recitation as the primary instructional activity seemed to rely on formal control sanctions and allocated most of their special assistance to the top-achieving pupils. In the other classrooms, by contrast, the teachers exercised more personalistic controls and provided considerable assistance to the children having most difficulty with class lessons. Besides these classroom-to-classroom variations, though, significant differences in teacher-pupil interactions also existed when different task activities were used by any one teacher. That is, regardless of teacher, control and assistance patterns varied with the type of instructional activity. In many ways, the task activity itself seemed to shape the teacher's behavior. In this chapter, the organizational arrangements of instructional activities, as they shape the teacher's action and the development of teacher-pupil relationships, will be analyzed.

Tasks, group management, and teacher authority

One of the most striking differences between the two third-grade classrooms (observed during the preliminary part of this study) was in the degree of teacher dominance over classroom events. Much of Ms. Hunt's activity in her classroom involved controlling her pupils. She was constantly checking to see whether every child had properly centered the title on his paper, calling for attention, or stopping children from talking out of turn during class discussions and recitation. Mr. Stone, on the other hand, spent much less time controlling his pupils' behavior. Differences between these two classrooms were reflected in the desist rates for each teacher. During the first six months of classroom observations, Hunt gave three times as many desists (i.e., a teacher's request for a child, group of children, or the entire class to stop an activity that violates classroom rules)[1] as Stone.[2]

Furthermore, the whole climate of each classroom seemed to reflect differences in the extent of teacher dominance over activities. Hunt was always the center of instruction in the classroom. She called only on children who had their hands raised, refused to continue when a pupil interrupted or was not paying complete attention, and constantly repeated or summarized children's answers to her questions. Even when her pupils were expected to work alone, Hunt always wrote a list of tasks on the board in the order they were to be completed and continually interrupted work activity to check which children had finished each assignment. In Stone's room, instruction was much less centered on the teacher. The children often were able to initiate and organize projects. And although Stone did not tolerate pupils interrupting him or others during a discussion, he did not make raised hands and constant attention mandatory. Whereas Hunt dominated her class by strict adherence to rules and regulations, Stone allowed his class a substantial amount of freedom and choice.

The traditional literature on teacher style would account for the differences between Hunt and Stone in terms of their basic personality differences. Hunt would be characterized as the "authoritarian" teacher, whereas Stone would be the "democratic" teacher.[3] This explanation of teacher authority and control assumes that certain teachers are inherently authoritarian or democratic, that those traits are part of their personality. Indeed, some of the differences between teachers may be traced to personality variables. However, when Stone used recitation, he also became much more control oriented than when he used class task and multitask activities. Likewise, Hunt relied somewhat less on desists than on individual or personalized control when she used multitask activities. If only observed during recitation, for example, both Hunt and Stone might be considered authoritarian teachers. Recitation activities, independent of the teacher, seem to demand a higher level of teacher dominance than multitask or class task activities. The amount of teacher dominance over classroom events and the use of certain types of control sanctions may therefore be related to the characteristics and usage patterns of classroom instructional tasks.[4]

Desists

Differences in teacher control behavior also were observed during the second year of the study. Both Ms. Hunt and Ms. Field, whose classrooms were dominated by the recitation activities, had significantly higher rates of desists than either Mr. Stone or Ms. Park (Table 4.1). At the same time, all of the teachers exhibited higher desist rates during recitation than during other instructional activities.

The high desist rates associated with the recitation indicate that this activity creates a fairly rigid control situation in which the teacher must sanction inappropriate behavior. As Jackson (1968) has pointed out, recitation demands a high degree of pupil attention. Pupils are supposed to listen to the teacher's question, understand it, and give the appropriate answer. Talking, reading, or drawing during the recitation decreases the child's ability to participate fully and learn the curriculum material. Furthermore, inattention can often lead to misbehavior that distracts fellow pupils from attending to the discussion.

[Recitation on social studies]

Field: Now, we know that the people don't have electricity.

Karen: (raises hand and is recognized by the teacher) They don't have any lights, either.

Field: What do they use at night to see what they are doing?

(Tim opens desk and pulls out a rubber ball which he rolls around on his desk behind his open book.)

(Field calls on Ann who has hand raised to answer.)

Ann: Candles and oil lamps.

(Fred sees Tim's ball and grabs for it. Mike looks over and says something to Tim, while Tim wrestles the ball away from Fred. Linda turns around to see what is happening.)

Table 4.1. *Desists per 100 minutes by activity type and teacher*

	Recitation	Class task	Multitask	Free	Organization	Total
Hunt	21.3	18.2	18.3	3.2	31.4	20.5
Stone	11.6	6.8	3.6	5.1	17.3	7.4
Field	23.0	17.1	14.5	6.2	24.0	19.3
Park	13.8	11.1	10.1	8.1	12.8	11.1
Average rate	17.4	13.3	11.6	5.7	21.4	14.6

Field: [Commenting on Ann's answer.]
   (Field notices the boys.)
Field: Boys, stop that. Tim put that away before I take it away.
You [Tim] shouldn't keep bothering Fred. You [Fred] need to
pay attention to this. Now, Fred, what do they use to see at night?
Fred: I don't know.
   Field: If you'd pay attention . . .

The teacher, then, must sanction misbehavior before it spreads to other
children and impedes the progress of the recitation.

Recitation also creates a situation in which surveillance of inappropriate behavior is optimal. During recitation, the whole class or, at
least, a large group is involved in the same activity. The teacher, who
usually stands at the front of the group, is able to observe each child's
behavior and detect most inappropriate actions – hence the high proba-
bility for such acts to receive desists. During class task and multitask
activities, particularly when the class is scattered over the entire room,
the teacher may never even see many acts of inappropriate behavior.

[Multitask work; two project groups working on murals, one
project group writing a short story; rest of the children reading
or writing stories on their own; children scattered into hall and
around the room, some in library.]
(Park working with one mural group. Helping them mix the
paints and prepare the brushes.)

(Kevin, who is working at desk, wads a piece of paper and throws
it out the open window. No one seems to notice him. He wads
another piece and throws it toward the window but mostly at
Linda who is reading at her desk. She looks at the paper but
ignores Kevin.)

(Park goes over to check on the progress of the other mural
group. She asks Debby if the drawing is going to fit with all the
rest of the birds. Debby says that she thinks it will. Park approves
a try.)

(Kevin in the meantime has begun writing again.)

Furthermore, pupils' ability to observe and be influenced by others'
misbehavior also varies with the task activity. Recitation was the only
instructional activity to contain a "ripple" of misbehavior, that is,
misconduct spreading from several pupils to the entire class.

[Math recitation]

Field: OK, now what is five in base two? Karen.

Karen: (hesitatingly) I don't know.

[Ms. Field explains the process, writing on the board with her back partly towards the children.]

(Robert and Terry are whispering to each other that Karen is a tomboy.)

[They are in different rows.]

(Laurie overhears them and says: "Tomboy schman boy. You're a tom-girl." Several others hear this and repeat "tom-girl" until nearly everyone is giggling and whispering that Robert is a "tom-girl.")

Field: (turning around from writing an equation on the board) What's the matter?

Laurie: Robert's a tom-girl. (Entire class laughs.)

Field: Watch your manners! Let's pay attention, all of you.

[Spelling recitation. Ms. Park reading words from a list and calling on children to come to the board and spell them correctly.]

(Ellen and Mary keep passing a note back and forth, using Tracy as an intermediary.)

[Recitation continues.]

(As Ellen passes note back to Mary, Kathy grabs the note, reads it, and hands it to Ted. Park doesn't appear to see this. Ted passes note to David. He reads it and passes it to George, who laughs.)

Park: What is this (going over to George and taking note)?

George: They just passed it to me (indicating Ellen and Mary).

Mary: No we didn't.

Park: You all know that you shouldn't do this. I don't care if you pass notes during your time, but we have a lesson to do. You need to pay attention, Ellen.

[Recitation continues.]

The task, then, by determining the size and publicness of the work group, influences the extent to which inappropriate behavior is visible to the teacher and fellow pupils. In a large group situation, like recitation, the opportunity for misbehavior to spread increases, as does the teacher's ability to detect misbehavior. This, coupled with the necessity for pupil attention in recitation, establishes a situation in which control becomes of prime importance. Misbehavior disrupts the recitation and must be sanctioned if class activity is to continue. However, when the task activity splits the class into small or individualized units, misbehavior usually does not affect other children's work, even if it is noticed. The recitation structure demands that the teacher deal with a large group, whereas multitask and class task activities entail the management of small groups or individuals within the classroom.

The equity of sanctions

. . . teachers face genuine dilemmas in resolving the conflict between appropriate treatment of individual children and the *demands of equity* [in leading a group of students]. In matters of discipline they must match their response to the personality of a student with the classroom rules they themselves have set up. Teachers act in fishbowls; each child normally can see how the others are treated. Teachers also learn they must create a system of rules early in the year and must behave consistently in terms of these rules [Lortie, 1975, p. 70, emphasis added].

The structure of task activities which, in part, determines the degree of visibility among members of a classroom also influences the sanctions that teachers use. For example, during multitask activities, a class is usually split into many different work groups. A teacher can provide special treatment to individual pupils without threatening the jural order of the classroom because such treatment is less visible to others when pupils are working separately. Mr. Stone and Ms. Park both said that they tried to fit their response to an event with the child's needs: Many rules applied to some children were not always applied to others.

> [Talking about differences between last year's group of pupils and this year's group]
> Stone: Last year's group also seemed a little more together. I really didn't have such a disparity in personalities.
> Researcher: In what ways?
> Stone: Well, take Karen and David [pupils in his current class]. Karen really needs someone to push her. Make her do the work. David had a hard time last year, really got turned off to working. He needs some space to relax. He'll do OK. But when he gets pushed, he freezes and refuses to do anything. So, I have to push Karen and ease off of David.
> Researcher: Like today when they were doing their work sheets?
> Stone: Yes, I knew David was goofing off and Karen, too. But, had

I come down on David, as I did with Karen, I wouldn't have gotten anything out of him.

This differential treatment was possible because it usually remained invisible to the rest of the class. This is not to say that the teacher in a multitask-organized classroom can be arbitrary in his application of classroom rules. Demands of equity surely exist when the teacher sanctions a child in the presence of others. However, the multitask organization allows teachers more freedom to handle misbehavior on an individual basis. Despite their often disparate application of the classroom rules, Mr. Stone and Ms. Park were thought of by their pupils as being very fair. Their extensive use of multitask activities allowed them to provide individualized treatment without upsetting the perceived jural order within their classrooms.

Recitation, however, because of its publicness, forces a teacher to be more impartial and consistent in his treatment of pupils. If a teacher were to provide special treatment to a child, the rest of the class would know. This would violate the rules the teacher himself established and would probably erode the trust or goodwill a teacher must have in order to gain the compliance of his pupils.[5] Furthermore, if the teacher were to stop the recitation, go over to the misbehaving child, and explain why the behavior was wrong, the rest of the class would likely start misbehaving while waiting for the teacher.

> [English recitation. John has been continually shouting out during the class time.]
> Field: What is the subject of this sentence?
> John: (shouting out) Man.
> Field: John, I've had enough of you this morning.
> [She walks over to his desk, leans down, and begins explaining why he shouldn't shout out.]
>
> (Carol begins whispering something to Linda. Debby turns around and joins into the conversation which erupts into giggling. Fred joins in, too.)
>
> (Field seems to hear the girls and looks up from talking to John.)
> Field: OK, now, that's enough. (walking to the front of the room) Now, what is the direct object of this sentence? And, raise your hands to answer.

Because recitation relies on the teacher as the main initiator of the activity, the entire class comes to a halt, at least in terms of instruction, when the teacher leaves his controlling position to deal with an individual child. Because of this, most teachers who rely on recitation use quick and impartial sanctions (usually a verbal or visual desist) to control their pupils.[6] *All of the teachers exemplified this pattern when using recitation activities.* They tended to sanction rigorously every violator of classroom rules.

One particular problem for all teachers is the child who constantly interrupts the progress of the recitation. Rather than stop to deal with the child's problem, the misbehaver is often expelled from the room until he can either return and "control himself" or until the teacher has an opportunity to talk to the child while the rest of the class is working on another type of task. The teachers expressed some concern that during recitation activities they were not always able to give the proper treatment to a child.

> [Conversation during recess]
> Field: Sometimes it's just too hard to give everyone what they need. I really didn't like sending John out of a room [during recitation], but he was causing such a nuisance. Disrupting the discussion and all. As you saw, he wouldn't even respond to my asking him to raise his hand if he wanted to answer. I really didn't have much choice. I couldn't just stop and talk to him.

Ms. Hunt tries to provide the personal attention children need by having periodic conferences with each child. However, this does not provide the immediate and special attention that a child may need.

> [Interview with Mr. Stone]
> Stone: I used to use a lot more structured things in my teaching. However, I felt I was being less responsive to each child. You know, when you're up there talking and trying to get the stuff across to the kids, it's really hard to handle each one's needs. That's why I like to be able to work with them . . . [W]hen I can immediately help them with their problems, things work out much better.

Again, it should also be noted that the use of impartial, quick controls is not a characteristic only of recitation-dominated classrooms like Ms. Hunt's and Ms. Field's. When Mr. Stone and Ms. Park used recitation in their classrooms, they also sanctioned children in ways similar to those of Hunt and Field – they became much more rigid and frequent in the control of their pupils. (See Table 4.1 for their higher than average desist rates during recitation.) Likewise, when Field used *multitask* activities, her control became much more individualized and adapted to each child. Her desist rate decreased significantly, and she utilized more personalized controls.[7]

Tasks and control

The task organization of an instructional activity influences the type of group management situation and, hence, the controls a teacher may use. The consistent pattern within each activity type *regardless of teacher* indicates that the task itself has considerable influence over the type of authority exercised in a given instructional situation. Recitation entails a standardized form and places the teacher at the center of control: Pupils' behavior is highly visible, as is the teacher's treatment of pupils. This visibility stimulates high desist rates and also creates "demands of equity" that force a teacher to rely on commands rather than on personal influence when controlling pupils. When the division of labor within the classroom is extensive, as in multitask organizations, the teacher does not control all activities. Each aspect of teacher and pupil behavior is less visible, allowing the teacher to use more personalistic and individualized means of control. The utilization of certain task activities, then, specifies the types of control and sanctions a teacher may employ. Classroom differences in the exercise of teacher authority reflect the exigencies of group management that are associated with different instructional organizations.

Teacher assistance and the academic hierarchy

Although particularistic treatment of pupils is limited by the use of institutional authority in control situations, recitation does not preclude the special treatment of pupils in all classroom situations. During the preliminary observations in the two third-grade classrooms, it was noted that certain pupils received considerably more opportunities to answer the teachers' questions. These pupils tended to be the ones who could answer most questions. In itself, this does not seem unreasonable: The brightest pupils would naturally be the most capable participants in a recitation. However, these pupils also received a disproportionate share of individual teacher assistance on their academic assignments despite the typical perception of teachers that most assistance is given to the least capable pupils. Although this assistance pattern existed in both Ms. Hunt's and Mr. Stone's classrooms during recitation, the most capable pupils did not receive the most assistance during multitask activities: Here, the least capable pupils received the most aid. Therefore, there appeared to be a relationship between the type of task activity and the allocation of teacher assistance among pupils.

At first, it seemed that teachers unconsciously allocated a certain amount of individual attention to each pupil. If the time was spent controlling the pupil, less time would be allocated to instructional assistance. Because recitation activities have the highest rates of teacher control and because pupils receiving the most desists were the least capable academically, the small amount of individual academic assistance given to the less capable pupils reflected their increased use of individual teacher attention for control purposes. However, further examination of classroom observation notes for all six classrooms indicated that this explanation could not account for differences in teacher assistance during different task activities – the amount of time required to control each pupil was very small. Even if the time spent controlling a child's behavior was added to each child's "share" of individual teacher assistance, differences in the total amount of special assistance allocated to each child remained.[8] The top-performing recitation pupils received the most teacher assistance. In order to explain this it was necessary to reevaluate the events in each classroom to see which pupils received special assistance, when they received it, and what consequences developed from differences in its allocation in each classroom.

Performance and assistance

During the first two weeks of school, all four teachers used many review tasks. Spelling, reading, and math were stressed in order to evaluate which children could do the work and which were having trouble. Even though the teachers had extensive records on I.Q. tests, achievement tests, and previous performance for each of their pupils, they did not rely on these data. As Ms. Park put it, "I have to see how they react to my class, not what their other teachers put in their cums [records]. After all, so much can happen over a summer." By the end of the second week, however, all four teachers had commented to the researcher that they could judge how well each child was going to perform, what problem they would have, and who would need extra assistance.

Two very different patterns of teacher assistance developed in response to this knowledge of pupils' capabilities. In the recitation-dominated classrooms, Ms. Hunt and Ms. Field began calling consistently on their top-performing pupils to answer the hardest questions. Nearly three of every seven questions were answered by the five top pupils. The top achievers also seemed to receive much more teacher attention than others in the class. For example, at the end of the second week of school, Field organized a group of four boys into a "math honor guard." These boys not only dominated math recitation by answering most (about 44 percent) of the questions, but they also received a large share of special instructional assistance and were allowed to work together while the rest of the class worked with Field.

[Math recitation]

Field: Oh, now this next problem is a hard one. [She writes an addition problem in base five on the board.] I think I need my math honor guard to demonstrate this one. Boys, up front. (David, Michael, Carl, and Eric come up front.) Can anyone tell them what to do [some raised hands]?

David: I know, I know.

Field: OK, you tell the rest what you want them to do.

David: [He has the other boys represent each of the numbers on their fingers, and lectures to the class how to add in base five.]

Field: That's good. I knew I could count on you. To your seats.

[Math recitation]

Field: That's excellent Michael. [He just answered a "hard" question.] You know (walking to the back row where all four "math honor guard" boys sit), you boys have done so well and answered so many questions today; I think you need to do something more challenging. You don't need to do this stuff anymore today. So, while I work with everyone else, I want you to figure out these problems. [Field spends five minutes giving them instructions while the rest of the class waits.] OK, you can do it – into the back of the room. OK, class (walking to front board) we have seven more minutes of these problems and then we can go to page . . . [recitation continues].

Ms. Hunt also favored several pupils who answered the most difficult questions and generally performed well on all task activities. Although she had nothing equivalent to the "math honor guard," Hunt did call on Erica, Lynn, and Janet to answer about twice as many questions as other pupils, especially during language and social studies. These three girls also were allowed to work together on extra assignments or special projects while the rest of the class worked alone or with Hunt. They completed about twelve of the seventeen special projects during the year.

Hunt and Field began relying on their top-performing pupils. During recitation, these pupils could keep the discussion going by answering the questions and demonstrating to the class that the material could be understood.

[Conversation during the fourth week]
Field: Now, Carl. I know I can rely on Carl to come up with the answers. He always thinks about what we're studying. He does his homework and really pays attention in class. Michael, too. They shine in all subjects. Even when no one else can get the question, I know Carl and Michael will – or, at least, they'll try.

[Conversation]
Hunt: I'm really pleased with this year. In general, I have a good group. A couple of problems, but not like last year. It was really difficult to get them to work as a group. You remember – sometimes it seemed like no one paid any attention to what was going on . . . I really don't have to worry this year with Lynn, Erica, Janet, and Patrick. Those four always come through. So enthusiastic – always ready to answer.

In relying on these pupils, Hunt and Field began using them as "standards" for performance in their classrooms. Because these top performers did the best work and usually could answer questions during recitation, their papers and answers became examples for the rest of the class.

[Ms. Hunt passing back stories the children had written the week before.]
Hunt: Oh, I really liked some of your stories. Some of you need a little work though. Like Martin (giving him his paper), you didn't space your words correctly. Look at this big space. Karen [handing back paper]. And, Kathy. Erica, an excellent job. [Ms. Hunt passes back more papers.] Now, I want the whole class to look at Lynn's paper. See how neat it is. The margins are all straight, and no spelling errors. A really good job. Why don't you come and read it to us Lynn. [Lynn reads her paper to the class.]

Hunt: If you want to compare your paper to Lynn's to see what an excellent job is, then you can ask her.

Field: (passing back folders with the children's work) If you really want to see what an exceptional job is look at Don's. I know I gave some of you excellents, but Don's folder is far better than anyone else's. [She opens the folder and displays Don's work, commenting on its excellence.]

However, the extra assistance that Hunt and Field provided these top-achieving pupils seemed to bolster the pupils' abilities to demonstrate competence in the classroom.

[Social studies recitation]

Field: Now, as we can see, these people have to work hard in the fields. What is it about the climate that makes farming so hard? (Only Carl raises his hand.)

I know you know it because you've read ahead. Can anyone else guess? Well, maybe not. Now Carl, tell the class what you know about the climate. I know this is hard because we haven't talked about it yet. But, you're the only one who read ahead. So try.

Fred: (aside to researcher) She wouldn't let me read ahead.

Carl: [Describes the climate.]

[Ms. Field asked Carl several questions, in all, taking four minutes of class time.]

Field: Thank you, Carl. [Recitation continues.]

The day before, Field had spent seven minutes with Carl while he was reading the extra section, asking him questions and generally explaining the text. Similar events occurred at other times in Field's and Hunt's classrooms. The top-achieving pupils were the only ones to receive this type of special assistance.

In the other two classrooms, this pattern of special assistance did not develop. Although Mr. Stone and Ms. Park did rely on certain pupils during recitation activities, these pupils did not receive additional assistance at other times; in fact, it was the least capable pupils who generally received the most individual assistance in their classrooms. For example, it was common for Stone and Park to split their classes into small project groups while they worked with a pupil or small group of children having difficulty on a task.

(Kids coming in from shop class – slowly get into seats – a lot of talking.)

Park: Uh-huh! Let me have your attention. Ellen sit down. OK, until music we're going to have an open period. If you need to finish anything, this is the time for it. Those who haven't yet done their math assignment for Ms. Anthony, this is the time to do it. Paul, I want to work with you. Bring your reading book.

[Rest of the class works alone on a variety of tasks. Ms. Park helps Paul with his reading for about sixteen minutes, then works with Tim, who is having trouble on his handwriting.]

Mr. Stone and Ms. Park spent most of every class task and multitask period helping the poorest pupils. If Stone and Park relied on their top performers, it was to organize their own work, leaving them free to give extra assistance to the less capable pupils.

[Conversation]

Park: I tend to depend on my best ones. [pupils] to be able to do their own work. You know this group of kids is pretty good at that. Terry and Albert don't need any help. They just start on a project and do it. When Terry did the mural, it was great. I didn't have to worry too much, it was their project.

I can spend more time with anyone having the problems. Like John. Oh, does he need help, but he's trying.

Rather than more teacher assistance, the top-performing pupils actually received less individual help in these two classrooms. In fact, in two-thirds of the multitask and class task periods observed, the top pupils received no individual assistance from their teacher. In Ms. Hunt's and Ms. Field's classrooms, the top pupils always received individual help.

Furthermore, the top-performing pupils rarely became standards for performance in Stone's and Park's classrooms. During class task activities, Stone and Park occasionally displayed the best papers or complimented the top achievers on their work. This was possible because every pupil was working on the same task. However, in multitask activities, pupils' accomplishments are seldom comparable because most of the children work on different tasks. Park noted that she often could not make comparative judgments about her pupils' achievements because of the number of different projects. Evaluation usually was based on how well each child was performing in relation to his own past performances and on the amount of effort. At one time or another during the year, every child had some piece of work displayed and praised publicly. This was not the case in either Hunt's or Field's classroom.

The task organization of a classroom, then, influences the allocation of teacher assistance to individual pupils. Because the teacher seems to depend, in part, on the top achievers during recitation, these pupils received a disproportionate share of individual assistance from the teacher particularly when they were beginning or completing extra assignments. This extra assistance actually enhanced the top-performing pupils' ability to retain their positions as "standards" for the class; they demonstrated that the material could be learned. In contrast, top-performing pupils in the multitask organized classrooms rarely received extra individual teacher assistance. Rather, they were expected to organize their own work, leaving the teacher free to assist pupils having the most difficulty with assignments. Because the task organization of the multitask classroom is characterized by a large number of different tasks being completed simultaneously, standards of performance for the entire class are often impossible to create. Hence no single child or group of children can become top achievers in every task activity.

What developed in the recitation-dominated classrooms was a teacher-organized academic hierarchy based on performance. An elite of top-performing pupils developed because special privileges, such as working in small groups and special projects, and teacher assistance were allocated in terms of a child's relative performance within the classroom. Because recitation and class tasks allow for comparative judgments of children's performances, Field's and Hunt's classrooms became differentiated in terms of pupils' performance levels. When asked to rate their pupils, Hunt and Field readily went down their class lists commenting on the performance level of each child. Park and Stone, however, had much more difficulty rating their pupils. Until he was asked to judge each pupil's own progress on specific skills, such as math, reading, and spelling, Stone commented that every one of his pupils was doing "academically sound" work. When Park rated her pupils, she said, "Oh, this is so hard. They change from one minute to the next. Some are good in reading, others math. I only have a couple who are good in everything. And, like I said before, it's really hard to tell since we're doing so many different things."[9] Because public, comparable evaluations of performance were minimal, these classrooms did not develop academic elites.

Tasks and the teacher-pupil relationship: a summary

The influence of classroom task organization on the teacher is quite apparent. Each task type comprises a social arrangement that shapes teacher behavior related to control and instruction, thus affecting teacher-pupil relationships that develop. The task structure influences the degree to which teacher and pupil behavior is public and activities depend on teacher control, and hence it creates differing control demands on the teacher. During recitation, pupils' behavior and the teacher's treatment of pupils are highly visible. This visibility, coupled with the teacher-centeredness of recitation, creates a situation in which sanctions must be equitable and impartial. In the multitask setting, by contrast, there are fewer "demands of equity" in sanctioning and the teacher can rely on personal influence to control his pupils.

The allocation of individualized instructional assistance also varied with task organization. In recitation, teachers rely on their top-performing pupils to facilitate the activity and demonstrate that the material can be understood. In the multitask setting, pupils cannot become standards for task performance because few tasks are assigned to the entire class. Even though all four teachers in this study felt that they provided the most individual assistance to the least capable pupils, this was true only of those two teachers who organized their classrooms around class task and multitask activities. The two teachers who predominately used recitation provided the most assistance to their top-performing pupils, thus bolstering those pupils' positions in the academic hierarchy of the classroom and ensuring their ability to perform well.

Teachers, then, must organize their behavior within the context of the particular structural properties of their work setting. In the classroom, the organization of instruction, in its effect on visibility, sanctioning, and task interdependence, creates a set of conditions to which a teacher must respond and, hence, shapes teacher-pupil relationships that develop.

5. Peer relations

In Harper School a variety of factors influenced pupils' selection of play- and workmates. As Tables 5.1, 5.2, 5.3, and 5.4 indicate, the children usually formed into friendship and work groups with seatmates of the same sex.[1] Children who had the same teacher during the previous year associated frequently at the beginning of the year, but this factor became less important in succeeding weeks as children made new friends. Race and neighborhood had some influence on friendship choice in Ms. Field's class; however, this was due primarily to two black children from the Lakeside area and to one pair of white boys from Parkwood who constantly associated with each other. And although neighborhood seemed to have some relationship to peer choices in Mr. Stone's room, this occurred because twenty-two of the twenty-six children resided in one area. Race and neighborhood did not influence friendship choice in Ms. Hunt's and Ms. Park's classrooms.

Once regular task activities began, however, differing patterns of peer relations emerged in these classrooms. As the school year progressed, the children in both Field's and Hunt's classrooms associated increasingly with children performing at similar levels.[2] In Park's and Stone's classrooms, however, achievement level did not affect friendship and work group choices. To what extent did differences in these classrooms' activity structures affect the patterns of peer association that emerged? As in industrial work groups (reviewed earlier), are peer relations influenced by the organization of work?

Tasks, competition, and academic status

In the recitation-organized classrooms, the emergence of academically homogeneous peer grouping paralleled the formation of academic elites (noted in Chapter 4). In Field's room, just as old friendships began to weaken, the math honor guard was created. Field encouraged its members to work together on math problems, and they soon began

63

Table 5.1. *Weekly summary of peer group composition: Ms. Field's classroom*

Week[a]	Number of		Children not in groups	Percent of groups homogeneous by					
	Groups	Changes		Sex	Race[b]	Neighborhood[c]	Classmates last year	Seatmates	Achievement level[d]
1	8	—	2	100	63	50	63	100	38
2	8	1	2	100	63	50	63	100	38
3									
4	7	5	3	100	71	58	43	85	58
5	6	2	4	100	67	50	17	83	67
6									
7	7	1	2	100	43	43	14	85	85
8	7	2	3	100	58	43	14	100	100
9									
10									
11									
12	7	3	3	100	43	58	29	100	71
13									
14	7	3	3	100	43	58	29	85	71
15									
16									
17									
18									
19									
20	7	3	3	100	58	58	14	100	85
21									

Note: Peer groups include those children who worked and played together. For comparable tables indicating play or work groups only, see Appendix B. Also see Appendix B for tables describing group composition changes by achievement level and the associations among race, sex, neighborhood, previous year's class, seatmates, and achievement level.
[a] Only weeks in which groups changed are noted. In a week where there were two changes, both are listed (see Table 5.4).
[b] Race was defined by visual inspection. The categories were Caucasian, black, and Oriental.
[c] Neighborhoods were indicated by the official, community named areas. The children lived primarily in two nonadjacent neighborhoods, Lakeside and Parkwood.
[d] Achievement level was defined by teacher ratings of each of their pupils. These occurred twice during the observation period.

Table 5.2. *Weekly summary of peer group composition: Ms. Hunt's classroom*

	Number of			Percent of groups homogeneous by					
Week[a]	Groups	Changes	Children not in groups	Sex	Race[b]	Neighborhood[c]	Classmates last year	Seatmates	Achievement level[d]
1	9	—	0	100	67	34	78	100	11
2									
3	9	5	3	100	45	45	33	100	33
4									
5									
6									
7									
8									
9									
10	10	4	1	100	50	50	30	90	60
11									
12	7	5	4	100	29	43	14	100	71
13									
14	7	1	5	100	29	43	14	100	71
15									
16									
17									
18									
19									
20									
21									

Notes: See Table 5.1.

Table 5.3. *Weekly summary of peer group composition: Mr. Stone's classroom*

Week[a]	Number of		Children not in groups	Percent of groups homogeneous by					
	Groups	Changes		Sex	Race[b]	Neighborhood[c]	Classmates last year	Seatmates	Achievement level[a]
1	7	—	4	100	29	43	86	100	29
2	7	4	2	100	29	43	58	100	29
3	8	6	3	100	50	75	50	87	25
4									
5									
6	8	6	4	100	63	75	38	100	38
7									
8	8	4	6	100	38	63	38	100	38
9	8	2	5	100	38	63	38	100	38
10	8	1	4	100	38	63	38	100	38
11									
12	7	8	5	100	43	71	29	100	29
13									
14	7	2	6	100	43	71	29	100	29
15									
16	9	7	3	100	33	78	22	100	44
17									
18									
19	7	2	4	86	58	71	29	100	29
20	9	4	3	100	67	78	44	100	33
21									

Notes: See Table 5.1.

Table 5.4. *Weekly summary of peer group composition: Ms. Park's classroom*

	Number of			Percent of groups homogeneous by					
Week[a]	Groups	Changes	Children not in groups	Sex	Race[b]	Neighborhood[c]	Classmates last year	Seatmates	Achievement level[d]
1	7	—	2	100	58	29	71	100	14
1	5	6	1	100	20	20	0	100	0
2									
3	8	5	1	100	25	50	38	100	25
4	7	3	1	100	29	58	43	100	14
5									
6	6	3	1	100	50	33	17	100	0
7									
8	7	4	0	100	43	14	50	100	29
9									
10	5	6	4	100	40	40	20	100	20
11									
12	7	3	3	100	58	58	43	100	14
13									
14	7	2	2	86	58	43	14	100	43
15									
16	7	2	3	100	58	58	43	100	14
17									
18									
19	7	3	1	100	29	58	43	100	14
20	7	3	1	100	71	58	43	100	14
21									

Notes: See Table 5.1.

eating and playing together during lunch and free time. In the fourth week of school, Carl, David, Michael, and Eric asked to have their desks moved together in the back of the room, forming a new row for the math honor guard. This allowed the boys to work together and talk without having to obtain Field's permission to use the back room. The move was one of the first in which pupils from different third-grade classes formed into a friendship group: Eric and David were friends in Hunt's room, and Carl and Michael were classmates in Stone's room.

During the fifth week of school, two other friendship groups emerged, mixing children from different third-grade classrooms. At the suggestion of Field, the two top performers on the independent reading laboratory (SRA) moved their desks together in the back of the room, away from the rest of the class.

> Don: (as he walks by to pencil sharpener) Tom and I are going to move our desks over here after lunch. Ms. Field wants us to.
> Researcher: Why are you moving?
> Don: Well, you see we're the two best on SRA. I skipped over to green and so did Tom, so Ms. Field wants us to work together on some of the exercises. Nobody else is that far. We can help time each other and correct them.

These two pupils occasionally played together before they moved their desks; however, *after* the move, they began to work and play together exclusively. Even when one of the boys wanted to play a game that the other did not like, the latter deferred in order to remain with his friend.

> [Ms. Field tells the class that they can have a 15 minute break.]
> Don: Let's go play checkers.
> Tom: Naw, I don't want to.
> Mike: (turning around in his seat) I'll play checkers.
> Don: I want to talk to Tom.
> (Tom and Don get up and look out the back windows, talking.)

Also during this week, three girls on the castle committee asked if they could move their seats together. Field approved because "they are good girls – they're sharp and they get their work done, not gab all the time."

By the end of the fifth week, then, nine of the ten top-achieving pupils had formed into three exclusive friendship groups. The only other performance-homogeneous group consisted of two "average-achieving" boys who had been best friends in Stone's room and who remained together throughout this year. In part, Field encouraged groupings among the top-performing pupils; they were the only ones who were allowed to work together while the rest of the class worked alone or with Field. These work group associations soon generalized: The pupils worked and played together during all activities within Field's class and in special classes as well. Gym was a notable exception for the boys. When the children were allowed to choose teams, the top boy athletes usually chose to play together regardless of academic performance level. After gym, however, the performance-homogeneous groups reformed.

During this period, the other pupils also began forming friendship groups based on academic performance. Because the top-performing pupils had already segregated themselves from others (sometimes physically by moving their seats away from the rest of the class), only the "average" and "poor" performing pupils remained free to interact. However, when Field did allow group work, she also encouraged the others to work with children performing at their own level. As with the top-performing pupils, this resulted in an increasing homogeneity of groups with respect to academic performance. For example, Frank, who had associated with David and Eric until they joined the other math honor guard boys, began eating, playing, and working with Fred and Patrick: All three were characterized by Field as "bright, but not consistent workers."

Play groupings were affected. For example, the split between Karen and Alice over Alice's joining two other friends from the castle committee (see Chapter 3) stemmed from Karen's need to finish assignments while the other girls played. Rather than continually fight to gain acceptance in an ongoing game, Karen withdrew from her long association with Alice and later began playing with Robert and Terry, who also had to spend much of their free time finishing assignments. But, after the seventh week of school, Karen never consistently worked with any group.

By the eighth week of the second year, all seven groups of children who normally worked, ate lunch, and played together consisted only of pupils achieving at the same level. Furthermore, these friendship groupings remained fairly constant throughout the remaining thirteen weeks of observations in this classroom. Although there were three changes, these did not alter significantly the achievement level composition of the groupings (see Table 5.1).

The emergence of friendship groups in Ms. Hunt's classroom was very similar to the patterns that developed in Ms. Field's. As the year progressed, the children began associating with others performing at the same level. By the end of the tenth week of school, six of ten friendship groups consisted only of academic "equals" (see Table 5.2). One of the crucial events influencing the emergence of academically based peer relations in this classroom was math grouping. In the seventh week, after Hunt separated the class into two groups for math instruction, several friendships dissolved. Friends who were placed in different math groups began associating more often with the children in their own math group than with their former friends. Anne, for example, who had been "best friends" with Karen since the beginning of second grade, soon began associating with Ellen after the two former friends were placed in different math groups. In all, three of four friendship groups that contained academic "unequals" separated during the three week period after the class had been grouped for math instruction.

Two characteristics of this classroom seemed to heighten the impact that math grouping had on friendship patterns. When Hunt split the class into math groups, she changed the seating arrangements so that children sat next to others in the same math group. This was done to "minimize the moving around to get settled for math." Because there were few occasions for the children to interact freely in this class (note the small amount of free time; see Table 3.2), most peer associations occurred between seatmates. By organizing the seating arrangement by math group, Hunt caused new patterns of association to develop among children achieving at the same level. Furthermore, because math was one of the few subjects during which children were allowed to work together, work groupings naturally formed only among children who had the same assignment. Children in different math groups could not work together. As in Field's room, these work associations usually developed into play associations, causing the increase in friendship groups based on academic performance level during the three weeks following math grouping.

Like Field, Hunt tended to allow only the top-performing pupils to work together on class assignments or special chores while the other pupils worked alone. When all the children were allowed to work together, Hunt usually selected the work groups so that children who were performing at the same level worked together.

Hunt: OK. You all can start work on this assignment. Remember

to do page 106 first (in math book). And, who knows what you do?
OK, Michael.
Mike: You head up a new sheet with title and name.
Hunt: Good. Now, you can work in pairs if you're quiet. OK, now.
(Children split up into pairs, some do work alone.)
Hunt: Announcement. I see that some of you are going to work
with someone in another math group. Well that isn't too good. So
please pick your partners from your own group. Amy and Laurie.
[Girls in different math groups – they separate and find new part-
ners as do the remaining children.]
Lynn and Erica, for example, became "best friends" while working on a
mural for their social studies project: Both were the top performers in
the class.

The emergence of friendship groups based on academic performance
in the recitation-organized classrooms seemed to reflect the importance
that achievement played in these classrooms. As a task activity, recitation makes pupils' performances public and comparable. Because the
entire class, or at least a large portion of it, works together during a
recitation, each child's performance is visible to both the teacher and
fellow pupils. If a child answers correctly, everyone knows because the
teacher usually praises the answer. However, if an answer is incorrect,
the recitation continues until someone produces the correct response.
As Jackson (1968) has pointed out, a pupil's self-esteem is constantly
challenged during recitation. When a child answers incorrectly, he may
receive both the disapproval of his teacher and the ridicule of his peers.
In a recitation class, the children know which of their peers are the
most capable just by their participation in the task.

In addition, demonstrations of performance often depend on others'
performances. During recitation, a pupil's ability to demonstrate his
knowledge and receive praise depends on others' answers. When another
pupil gives the correct answer, a child cannot show that he also knew
the answer for that question. In these classrooms, children often tried
actively to get the teacher to call on them; they raised their hands high,
sat up in their seats, and said aloud that they knew the answer.

[Work sheet correction]
Hunt: Now who wants to answer question 3?
(Raised hands)
OK, Kim.
Kim: It's . . .

Hunt: (interrupting) Read the whole sentence Kim.

Kim: A principal highway is marked by a single red line (several of the kids jump up and down in their seats, raising their hands and saying, "no, no").

Hunt: There seems to be some disagreement. OK, Martin. (Martin is just about standing behind his desk with his hand raised.)

Martin: Phew! It's a red and black line.

Hunt: Read the whole sentence Martin.

Martin: A principal highway is marked by a red and black line.

Hunt: Good. Kim look at your map again and see. OK.

Task performance, therefore, depended in part on fellow pupil's performances and one's ability to answer the teacher's questions during recitation. In this way, recitation creates a competitive situation.

Rather than compete against every other pupil in the class, though, the top-performing pupils formed support groups that helped each other on assignments. As one of Field's pupils said, "You need smart friends in the fourth grade. The work is harder than in the third, and you have to count on someone to help." These groupings were reinforced by Hunt and Field because only the top performers were allowed to work together at the first of the year.

[Social studies recitation]

Hunt: Well, Erica and Lynn you've just really understood this reading well. Why don't you two go back and work on the board [bulletin board] in the back room. Let me help you get started. [Hunt shows the girls where the paper and alphabet stencils are – spends about 3 minutes helping them start. Meanwhile the rest of the class is talking.] OK now class. Let's cut the talking, we still have work to do.

When the rest of the children were allowed to work together, they also formed into academically homogeneous groups. Following the top performers, the average pupils began working and playing together, leaving the poorer pupils to work alone or among themselves.

[Conversation, eighth week]

Frank: Look at those guys. [Robert and Terry are wrestling on the rug. Everyone else is working in groups on math assignments.] They're stupid.

Researcher: I thought you liked Robert. [After David and Eric formed a friendship group with Michael and Carl, Frank joined Robert, Terry, and Andrew.]

Frank: I did, but they goof off too much. Look at them. Pat and Fred are better friends. We can all work together – on SRA and stuff.

Because many of the special privileges in Field's and Hunt's classrooms were allocated on the basis of task performance, it became important for most of the children to finish their assignments on time and do their best work. The formation of academically homogeneous groups allowed the children to help each other, thus increasing their ability to obtain rewards. Children who associated with others achieving at lower levels often could not take advantage of their performance. For example, even though Laurie was often excused from recitations in Field's class because of her consistent high performance, she usually sat at her desk waiting for her girlfriends while the rest of the top achievers played or worked on other projects in their own groups. For most children, the rewards derived from task performance were sufficiently salient to cause them to join friendship groups that helped them perform and enjoy their rewards (such as extra free time) collectively.

During interviews with the fourth-grade children from Field's room, twelve of the twenty-three pupils specifically mentioned academic performance as a criterion for selecting friends.

[Interview]
Andrew: I can't goof around too much. If I do, my work don't get in on time. You see Robert. I don't want to be like him. Ms. Field is always on him to work harder. I want to be on the castle committee, too.

[After the twelfth week, Andrew stopped working with other groups. He worked on his own and was described by Ms. Field as "one of the few kids who has made real progress." He was considered a poor performer.]

Carl: I really like the group this year.
Michael: We all like each other.
Carl: You see we are all withdrawn from the class so that we can work better. [Referring to the four "math honor guard" boys who formed their own row.]
Michael: If one is absent, we can go to another for help.
Carl: Friends are good to have.
Michael: So many of the kids like the people in the back row [math honor guard boys], and everyone wants to sit back there.

Carl: We're the smart set.

Michael: Like Fred. He wants to sit by Carl.

Carl: Yeah, he keeps moving his desk back by us and wants to work with us on math problems and stuff.

Researcher: Don't you like Fred? He was one of your best friends last year [in Mr. Stone's class].

Carl: Well, he's OK, but he doesn't do his work that much. We want to keep our row together as the best.

Michael: He goofs off.

Jan: I don't like David because he brags about his SRA too much.

Carol: He says he's going to skip to gold. Ha!

Jan: I mean it's OK to do well. That's why I like Debby and Karen. They can help you. They're smart like David too, but they don't brag as much.

   [Carol, Debby and Jan are considered average students.]

The third-grade children also mentioned the importance of academic performance when selecting work and play partners.

Erica: Let's go play the flash cards.

Lynn: No, Sue is playing with them.

Erica: So.

Lynn: She's so dumb. She isn't even on page 100 yet [in the math book].

Laurie: George thinks he's so smart just because he got a 100 [George sits next to Laurie].

Sue: We don't need him! You can come over by me.

Laurie: Yeah. We can work together.

However, several children in each class were not concerned with the academic performance level of their friends. In Field's class, Laurie continued to associate with three girls who were performing at a lower level even though she often had to wait for them to finish their work or work alone when Field separated the class into task groups. Karen just withdrew from most peer relations when she and Alice separated. Likewise, Jenny withdrew from peer relations when her seat was moved away from Ellen's, and Ellen began associating with others in the same math group. However, Kevin and Scott continued their two-year friendship even though they sat in different rows after Hunt had placed them in separate math groups. Not all of the children, then, were concerned with the academic performances of peers, though most were.

As Thibaut and Kelly (1959) have indicated, status systems within a group emerge when group members are affected by the actions of others. Status systems based on competitive relations among pupils seem most likely to develop in classrooms where pupils observe and are affected by others' performances. This was the case in both Field's and Hunt's classrooms. Their extensive use of recitation and class task activities, such as tests, work sheets, and common assignments, allowed pupils to compare their task performances. The children knew their peers' achievements and constantly compared their performances. Comparisons were important because success in these classrooms depended on other pupils' performances; recognition and rewards, such as the math honor guard and castle committee, were based on a child's performance in relationship to the entire class. Rather than compete against everyone, the top-performing pupils in these class-rooms tended to form friendship groups that provided academic support. These groups were encouraged because only the top performers were allowed to work together on assignments and given extra free time and assistance. Associations during task activities soon generalized to play situations as well, creating achievement-homogeneous friend-ship groups among most of the top performers. When the entire class was allowed to work in groups, the average pupils also began choos-ing to work with children achieving at their same level. In part, this was a consequence of the task structure. Because everyone progressed at a different rate through the common assignments, the children were usually at different stages in completing their work. Hence it was natural for children to work with others who progressed at the same pace: Children could not work with peers who were on a dif-ferent SRA level or in another math group. The groups formed dur-ing task activities remained together during all other activities, thus creating the performance-homogeneous peer structures observed in these classrooms.

Unlike group patterns in Ms. Hunt's and Ms. Field's classrooms, achievement level (as identified by the teacher) did not effect the friendship group choices of Mr. Stone's and Ms. Park's pupils.

Only three of the eight friendship groups in Stone's class during the tenth week consisted exclusively of academic equals. Because the predominant type of activity in his class was class task, the pupils knew how well their fellow classmates were performing on some tasks. Comments were often made on a child's speed or lack of it in com-pleting a work sheet, but this seemed to produce little competition because work sheets were not graded and the children usually worked together.

[Class working on work sheets – alone and in pairs]

Rick: (turning around to Don and Bob) I bet Tom and I can beat you. We're already on number six.

Bob: Who cares.

Rick: We're fastest.

Don: This isn't a race Rick. We're just taking our time.

Stone did not give special privileges to children who finished quickly or had the best score; but he did praise the top performance on most class tasks.

Furthermore, as the number of multitask activities increased throughout the year, the children in this classroom became involved in tasks that were neither comparable nor public. This decreased the opportunities to make performance comparisons, because the children worked on a variety of different tasks. These multitask activities also increased the opportunities for children to interact freely in a variety of task situations. Rather than encouraging those performing at similar levels to work together, multitask activities encouraged children to choose groups according to their interest in the task. It was not uncommon for children who were considered "best friends" to do different tasks during multitask activities, and this often led to the shifting of friendship group membership.

[Math recitation finishes.]

Stone: OK, let's begin those reports.

(Kids get out paper and split into small groups. Tom, Bob, Rick, Scott, and Paul all gather by Tom's desk. Talking.)

Stone: What are you doing?

Bob: We're trying to decide groups.

Stone: I thought you had it worked out yesterday. You told me Tom, Rick, and Bob were going to work together. And, Scott and Paul were going to.

Scott: Well, Paul wants to change. He likes their topic better.

Stone: Well?

Tom: I'm going to work with Scotty.

Stone: That's OK, just get some work done. I don't care what the groups are.

[Two days later, Tom moved his desk up by Scott and Paul moved back by Bob and Rick.]

Whereas peer groups in Hunt's and Field's room remained quite constant after the tenth week of school, friendship groups constantly changed in Stone's room: In eleven weeks, there were two changes in Hunt's, three in Field's, and nine in Stone's classroom.

Academic performance occasionally was a criterion for friendship and work groups in Stone's classroom, particularly when the task was to be graded. During the sixteenth week, for example, four girls formed a friendship group and moved their desks together because they were "the tops in spelling and handwriting." This occurred during the period Ms. Kay, the student teacher, was instructing the class in these two subjects (see Chapter 3). Kay primarily used recitation and announced who was doing the best work, referring to the task of completing spelling and handwriting exercises as a race; and she allowed only the top-performing pupils to work together on these exercises. This stimulated substantial competition and resulted in the formation of the friendship among the four top-performing girls. After Kay finished her lessons, the importance of performance decreased, and the girls later separated into different groups. However, most of the time Stone's pupils willingly worked and played with most of the other children in their class.

Peer relations in Park's classroom also were fluid and independent of relative academic performance. No more than three friendship pairs (of seven or eight groupings) contained only academic equals. Because peer groupings constantly shifted in this classroom, nearly every pupil belonged to a friendship group with every other pupil of the same sex at least once during the year. The only exception was two girls who remained a cohesive pair throughout the year. Park's children seemed to change friendship groups as often as interests in projects or hobbies changed. During the period this class was observed, the children initiated nineteen seating changes due to shifts in friendship groupings, approximately one per week. The children in Stone's class initiated twelve shifts; there were seven such shifts in Field's class, and four in Hunt's class. Illustrative of the fluidity of peer associations in Park's class was the formation and subsequent dissolution of the Nancy Drew Mystery Book Club (see Chapter 3). Two seating shifts established the club among six girls, while one change reflected its demise into three separate pairs. Other shifts occurred when groups formed among several boys who played war games during free-time periods, among football fans during that season, and among children having common task interests. Because there were often many different tasks going on at the same time, Park's children could easily change groups when they became uninterested in a project.

[Multitask]

Ellen: (going up to Park) Ms. Park, I really don't want to work on the mountain (project building a papier-mâché mountain).

Park: OK, Ellen. What do you want to do?

Ellen: I think I'd like to paint.

Park: OK, go over by Terry and Kathy and get started. They can help you.

The multitask activities allowed a freedom of choice that did not exist in the recitation-dominated classrooms. The children themselves were responsible for selecting and organizing many of their tasks.

Multitask activities do not allow for the observation and comparison of task performance among pupils, so that achievement rarely became a concern in peer relations. Few children completed the same task, and when they did, task performance never became a criterion for special privileges. There was no math honor guard or castle committee. It made little difference who had finished their work first or who was ahead in their language booklet. When the children did work together on common tasks, such as a math assignment or spelling, they did not form into performance-homogeneous groups. In fact, when Park often asked children to help each other on assignments, she did so with little regard for the pupils' academic performance levels.

[Conversation]

Park: My kids have to be able to work together. Things really don't go well otherwise. I can't police one group while I'm working with another. It's good that I have several helpers this year. Terry is so good. She doesn't boss the kids and can really help on some things. Though, it was funny the other day – you weren't here – to see Ted helping Charles with his math. Talk about the blind leading the blind.

Within this classroom there was very little competition. Occasionally, some comments were made about a pupil's achievements in math, spelling, and on the language booklets. However, this rarely seemed to affect other friendship choices. In all, these pupils were open about their achievements and failures. For example, at the end of every spelling test Park would give two "hard" words not on the regular spelling list. None of the children seemed afraid to share their performance on these "hard" words with their classmates, even if they spelled both words wrong. This was different from the competition in both Hunt's and Field's classrooms.

[Spelling test]
Park: OK, now for the hard words. The first one is "dictionary." I looked up the word in the "dictionary." The next one is "establishment." This is a good "establishment."
(Kids write down words.)
OK—
Ellen: Spell the hard words. (Several kids say how many they think they got right.)
Park: "Dictionary" is d-i-c-t-i-o-n-a-r-y. "Establishment" is e-s-t-a-b-l-i-s-h-m-e-n-t.
Ellen: Yeah, I got them both.
[Kids discuss how many they got right.]
Mike: Oh, I only got one.
Ted: Well, I tried anyway.

[Checking math homework – Hunt's class]
After every answer she gets correct, Laurie cheers and waves her hands over her head.
Laurie: (to George) How many are you getting right?
George: None of your business. (He covers his book.)
Laurie: Let me see. (She tries to uncover his hands over the book.)
George: You don't need to know.
Laurie: Well, I got every one right so far.

[Lunch – Field's class]
Fred wanders up to the SRA box and starts looking through, commenting on the progress of everyone else. He laughed at Mark's booklet because Mark is only on red [the first level].
Only one pupil in Park's classroom mentioned academic performance in selecting friends: He was a pupil in Hunt's class the year before. Because there was little competition, few children were categorized by their peers in terms of performance levels. Two exceptions were Terry and David. Terry's art skill was recognized by everyone in the class, and David was aptly called the "math brain." However, these distinctions were much more task specific than comments made by the children in Field's and Hunt's classrooms, where the children rated each other in very general performance categories, like "top," "average," and "stu-

pid." Terry's and David's distinctions, moreover, did not hinder them from working with anyone else in the class. Most of the children agreed with the statement one boy made, that "the kids in this class are mostly nice and friendly. I get along well with them, and have fun. You help each other when you can."

Interesting to note are the similarities and differences in patterns of peer associations exhibited among the thirty-five children who experienced similar or different classroom task structures over the two years of this study. In the third grade, these children all tended to follow the patterns described earlier. Pupils in Stone's room were willing to associate with most of their fellow classmates, and peer groupings changed frequently. Children in Hunt's room formed friendship groups that remained very stable and reflected the academic performance hierarchy within the class. Among those children who went from Stone's room to Park's or from Hunt's to Field's – classrooms having similar activity organizations – there was little change in the patterns of the peer associations. Stone's pupils continued to be involved in a variety of friendship and work groups without regard for academic performance, whereas Hunt's pupils still associated primarily with children of similar achievement levels. However, children who were in a fourth-grade classroom with a different task structure exhibited considerable changes. In Park's room, Hunt's former pupils became less competitive and began associating freely among fellow pupils. Stone's former pupils, who had been very cooperative the previous year, became increasingly concerned with their academic performance in Field's room and began associating exclusively with children performing at their same level.

In Park's class, only one of the seven children from Hunt's room continued to evaluate peers in terms of their achievement level.

[From conversation]

Jim: Yeah, the kids in this class are pretty smart, I guess. No real dumb ones, except maybe for Ned. I like to work with guys that can help you. I don't like giving away all the answers.

However, because the top performers in Park's class usually worked and played with average and poor performers, Jim often was not involved in a friendship or work group except when he and Donald (another top performer) occasionally worked together. Other children dropped their performance-homogeneous groupings soon after entering

Park's class. For example, the three top-achieving girls from Hunt's room comprised a uniform group during the first week, but this group quickly dissolved when one of the girls joined a new, nonhomogeneous friendship group and the two others played with an "average achiever" from Stone's class. Most of the children in Park's room chose friendship groups without regard to others' performance levels, even those who had been extremely competitive the year before.

In Field's class, by contrast, the children who had worked and played with most of their classmates the year before began to associate exclusively with pupils performing at the same level. Carl, for example, who played checkers and traded stamps with anyone in Stone's third grade, only associated with his math honor guard friends the next year.

[Lunch]
(Andrew comes over to Carl and asks him if he would like to play checkers. Carl says no – that he and Michael are going to play after they finish eating. Andrew asks Peter who agrees. Carl, Michael, Eric, and David [the math honor guard boys] just stand near the windows looking out and talking.)
[Andrew is an average pupil.]

Except for Alice and Paul, who did not become involved in regular work and play groups, all of Stone's pupils formed performance-homogeneous friendship groups with their classmates in Field's room.

The shifting importance of academic performance in choosing friends was noted by the children themselves.

[From pupil interviews]
Karen: I don't like those boys who sit in the back [the math honor guard]. Carl was OK last year [in Mr. Stone's class], but now he's so stuck up. You know he won't even trade [stamps] with anyone now. And, David too. [Karen is an average performer.]

Lisa: I really like this year [in Ms. Park's room]. The kids are more friendlier. Last year I didn't have too many friends. Ms. Hunt didn't let us work together very much. I like working with Terry, doing art. [Lisa is an average performer.]

Dan: David and I were good buds last year [in Ms. Stone's room]. But not now [in Ms. Field's].
Researcher: Don't you still ride the bus together [from Lakeside]?

Dan: Yeah, but since he's got on the castle committee, we don't. They all hang together at lunch and everything. Won't let anyone in.

Even parents and teachers of special classes commented on changes as the children went from one type of class to another.

[Conversations]

Parent (of boy who had Mr. Stone and Ms. Field): His mother and I noticed how much more concerned he is about doing well. At the dinner table, it is always talk about who is on the castle committee, who got kicked off because they didn't finish their homework, who is on what color in SRA, and the like. I really wasn't aware of this last year. Much more competition this year.

Language Teacher: Kathy was tremendously competitive last year [in Ms. Hunt's class]. She wouldn't work with anyone but Alice [another top performer]. She'd ridicule others. Now [in Ms. Park's room] she's teacher's helper – quite a switch. Very willing to work in groups. Since she picks up things fast, she's a good teacher.

Counselor: We've noticed a real shift in Ned. He was so withdrawn – no real friends [last year in Ms. Hunt's class]. We think that he didn't function too well in peer groups. This year he is much better. You notice how active he's become [in Ms. Park's class] and he's got several friends too.

Ms. Park tells me that he's going to blossom soon.

[Ned is a poor achiever.]

Tasks and peer relations

The consistency in forms of peer group structures, both between classrooms having similar instructional organizations and within the same classroom over the two-year study period, as well as the friendship shifts that occurred among students who changed classroom types, demonstrates the impact of the organization of instruction. The varying importance that academic performance played in the selection of friends and workmates cannot be attributed to differences among the children. These pupils adapted readily to the influence of task and reward structures and responded to the dominant organization present in their current classrooms.

The structure of recitation allows for individual comparisons and when accompanied by comparative assessments of performance, fosters the development of a competitive status system within the classroom. Status and interpersonal bonding depend on individual performance. This decreases overall group cohesion and reinforces social relationships that support both the pupil's productivity and chances for obtaining rewards. In recitation-organized classrooms, children separate into performance-homogeneous friendship groups that remain exclusive and fairly stable throughout the year. By contrast, the structure of the multitask organization does not involve comparative assessments of pupil performance. Status, based on academic achievements, and competitive peer interactions do not develop. Pupils are free to establish a variety of social relations without regard for their instrumental value in obtaining performance recognition. They choose friends and work-mates often on the basis of task or hobby interests, changing groups as their interests shift.

One consequence of these different patterns of peer associations in the four classrooms was the extent of cooperative behavior among pupils. Most of the children in both Mr. Stone's and Ms. Park's class-rooms were willing to work with each other in groups. In Ms. Hunt's and Ms. Field's classrooms, by contrast, the competitive attitude of the children, particularly the top achievers, resulted in segregated work groups according to performance level. Although it was common to see a top-performing pupil helping or working with a low-achieving pupil in either Stone's or Park's rooms, the children in Hunt's and Field's classes rarely worked with children other than those in their academically homogeneous friendship groups. Field herself commented that her pupils "did not seem to know how to work together as a group." Ironically, two of the pupils she considered most uncoopera-tive with the other children seemed able to work in a small group the preceding year in Stone's classroom.

6. The impact of task organization

It might be said that the teacher is the most important influence on the emergence of social relationships in a classroom. Even if the organization of tasks provides the setting in which pupils and teachers interact and social relationships are formed, it is the teacher, after all, who first chooses activities and specifies how these will be evaluated. Although certain tasks, like recitation, influence the types of sanctions that can be employed and involve a high level of teacher control over classroom activities, teachers who are "naturally" authoritarian may choose to use a high proportion of recitation in their classrooms. Likewise, teachers who are less dominative may choose the multitask organization. Rather than being totally emergent within the context of the task setting, social relationships develop in response to the teacher's choice of activities.

But this is true only in part. Indeed, it is the teacher who usually (though, not always) chooses task activities.[1] However, once this choice is made and task activities are instituted, the social relationships that develop are somewhat outside the teacher's control. This became quite evident when Ms. Field tried to change the activity structure in her classroom.

Ms. Field's change

After the Christmas break, Field expressed dissatisfaction with some of the pupils in her class. She had received several complaints from the music teacher (whose room was next door) about the amount of noise her class made during free time. Although Field told the music teacher that her children needed some free time to "get out their energies," she also mentioned to several other teachers that her class was unruly and most of the children could not work together as a group.

[Conversation]

Field: I just don't know what is the matter with this class. They really don't know how to cooperate. They're always fighting, kicking, pinching. No manners at all. If I try to work with one child alone, the whole class erupts. There are some that I just cannot trust to turn my back on. They just really need limits.

As one counselor who often visited Field's room said, "Her class just seems to explode when she lets them have a break." Indeed, whenever Field scheduled free time after a period of instruction, most of the children would jump up from their seats and race to the carpet to play, wrestle, and talk to their friends. Field needed the help of a bell or whistle and often a yardstick held in a threatening manner to get her pupils to their seats at the end of a free period.

Several of her fellow teachers, including Ms. Park, suggested that Field try splitting her class into smaller groups and allow the children to organize their own projects; in other words, she should try to use more multitask activities, which is, in fact, what Field did. During the seventeenth week of observations, Field began using considerably more multitask activities. She had several periods when most of the children were allowed to choose and organize their own group projects, such as group reports in which the children picked their own topics. In a fourteen-day period, Field increased her use of multitask activities from 13 to 31 percent and decreased recitation from 44 to 24 percent of the total classroom activities. (Class task activities remained at 24 percent.)

In addition, she began ignoring many of the acts of misbehavior that she normally would have sanctioned.

> [Conversation]
> Field: Did you see what Robert did today?
> Researcher: Yes. [He grabbed Tom and threw him to the floor.]
> Field: I really don't know what to do. I'm trying to ignore a lot of stuff. Maybe they'll get it out of their systems. I don't know. I just don't like it. I talked with [the principal] and he doesn't know what to suggest either. I guess I'm just going to let it go on for a while and see what happens.

Rather than immediately sanctioning a child who was talking loudly or bothering another pupil, Field waited to see whether the misbehavior would stop before she gave a desist. During this period, Field's total desist rate dropped from nineteen to ten desists per hundred minutes of class time (cf. Table 4.1).

In this fourteen-day period, the task organization of Field's classroom became very similar to that of Park's: Both were multitask organized. Field and the teachers who suggested the change hoped this use of multitask activities would allow the children an opportunity to work together, making the children realize that cooperative activity was possible.

However, the change in the task organization in Field's classroom failed to produce the expected results. First, many of the children seemed to view small group projects as opportunities to socialize with their friends. Since the nine top-performing pupils usually were the only ones allowed to work together before this change, most of the other children had not had the opportunity to work in small groups outside of Field's watchful eye. The times in which these pupils could interact was during free time. Therefore, it seemed that the major portion of every project period was spent talking or playing with friends, rather than working on the project. On the first group report, Field had to extend the completion deadline twice to accomodate talkative groups. During this period, Field's class did not operate as Park's did. Many of the children were unable to work quietly and cooperatively in small groups.

[Conversation]

Field: It's not going well.

Researcher: In what way?

Field: Well, I want them to cooperate. But all they seem to do is chatter and fight. Some are OK. Carl, Michael, Jory – you know the bright kids. But the rest. I just don't know. When they get in groups, nothing seems to get done but playtime.

Second, in Park's class, the top-performing pupils usually worked in different groups during multitask activities. This was important because these pupils often helped the others, leaving Park free to work with children having the most difficulty. However, when Field instituted more multitask activities, the top performers in her class remained together in their own solidary groupings. The boys from the math honor guard, for example, would not let anyone else join their work group. Even when Field asked Carl to work with another group of boys in order to help them get started on one project, Carl soon returned to his original group of top performers.

[Small group work. Reports. Carl comes up to Field, who has been talking to the researcher.]

Carl: Ms. Field. I just can't be in that group anymore.

Field: Why not? They need your help.

Carl: But, they just want to goof off.

Field: You can help show them how to begin the report, yours was excellent last time.

Carl: I'd rather work with Michael and Eric.

Field: Well, OK. Since we just have 13 minutes more left, you go back and work with Peter and Robert, and go back with them [Michael and Eric] tomorrow.

In part, these events seemed due to the fact that friendship groups had already developed in this classroom. The class had become differentiated along achievement lines, and work groups reflected this performance stratification. In Park's room, the children chose project groups based on their interest in the project. However, the children in Field's class chose their groups and then tried to organize a project. This often created a problem in trying to find a topic or task acceptable to everyone in the group.

[Class split into small groups, working on reports]

Tom: (coming up to the researcher, followed by Don and Ned) What should we do for our report?

Researcher: I don't know. What do you want to do?

Ned: We can't decide. Why don't you help us? We need a topic.

Researcher: What are you interested in?

Tom: I want to do something on space travel, but these guys don't want to.

Ned: I want to do money.

Tom: Oh, that's not interesting, what can you do about it?

Ned: I don't know.

Researcher: What do you want to do Don?

Don: I like the money idea.

Researcher: Well, why don't you and Ned do money, and Tom you can go work with Robert and Bruce. They're doing something on space travel.

Tom: I don't want to. Anyway we're working together.

Ned: Yeah, we want to do a report with Tom.

[Ned, Tom, and Don are above average achievers – Robert and Bruce are low achievers.]

Furthermore, the competitive structure of this classroom influenced the extent to which top performers were willing to help others.

[Class working in small groups on reports]

Carl: (coming over to SRA box – by researcher) Did you see John? He's working with George and Al. Doing everything.

Researcher: He's helping them.

Carl: Yeah, doing all the work himself. Those guys couldn't write a report by themselves if they tried. He should let them do it themselves.

Later, Carl complained to Field. When the second group project was organized, Field asked John to work with another group because he had done most of the work on the last report and she wanted "to see how George and Al do on their own."

Third, Field was not able to provide additional assistance to the groups of pupils who were having the most difficulty. Even though she tried to distribute her assistance among groups equally, the top-performing pupils still commanded much of her attention.

[Multitask]

(Carl, Michael, and Eric are clustered around Field's desk. She is working with Karen on math.)

Field: You boys go away. You can do your own work.

Carl: We need to ask a question.

Field: I'm too busy. I need to work with Karen.

Eric: But we can't go on.

Field: Think it over. Well, OK. What is it?

[Field spends 6 minutes helping the boys on an extra problem, not part of any assignment. Karen received about 4 minutes of assistance on an assigned exercise with which she was having trouble.]

These top-performing pupils had received most of Field's attention in the past and seemed to expect more attention during multitask activities as well. In the other multitask-organized class, by contrast, the top-performing pupils were expected to work without extra teacher assistance.

In all, the shift in activities did not produce a corresponding shift in social relationships in Field's classroom. The patterns of interaction that developed during the recitation-dominated period remained even after the multitask organization had been adopted. Field's pupils still expected her to be in control of the class.

[Conversation]

Jory: I don't like all these projects. I wish Ms. Field would be teaching again.

Researcher: Why don't you like the projects and reports?

Jory: Well, you know. So many of the kids are just goofing off. There's so much noise. And, Mark slapping everyone on the behind. I wish Ms. Field would tell him to stop it. She's the teacher.

At the end of the nineteenth week of observations in this classroom, Field decided that the multitask organization was not working. Subsequently, she returned to the recitation-dominated organization for the remainder of the year.

As this example illustrates, teachers themselves are constrained by their initial choice of instructional activities. Once stable patterns of interaction develop within the context of one task organization, subsequent changes in task activities seem to have little impact. There is, then, a "feedback" within the classroom: Social relationships that emerge as a result of a particular task organization influence the types of tasks that can be utilized within the classroom and, hence, reinforce existing patterns of sanctioning, authority, assistance, and peer associations.

Tasks and social relationships: a summary

The organization of instructional activities does affect the social relationships that develop within classrooms. The work arrangements of an instructional task not only shape the patterns of interaction among persons engaged in that task but also influence the development of social relations within classrooms that rely predominantly on that activity. In analyzing classroom tasks, several basic properties emerge: Activities differ in terms of the size of the work group, the number of different tasks in progress at the same time, the extent of pupil choice over the task and its completion, and the way in which task performance is evaluated and rewarded. Using these variables, three types of task activities can be identified – recitation, class task, and multitask – and elementary school classrooms themselves can be characterized by their relative usage of these instructional modes.

In classrooms employing different task organizations, different patterns of interaction emerge. Between teacher and pupils, for example, patterns in the exercise of authority and the allocation of assistance varied by task utilization. During recitation, all four of the teachers displayed relatively high desist rates and used impartial and impersonal means of controlling pupils. These qualities are constitutive elements of the work organization of recitation, which creates a group management situation in which teacher and pupil behavior is public and pupil attention is necessary for the smooth operation of the task. Because recitation places the teacher at the center of instruction, he is able to observe most misbehavior and tends to rely on quick commands to sanction it. If a teacher attempts to treat a child individually during recitation, he may lose control of the entire class, waste instructional time, and violate the demands of equity. During multitask-organized activities, by contrast, the teacher need not control the entire class at once. Because the children are separated into smaller groups or are working alone, the teacher need only monitor pupil behavior periodically. If misconduct occurs, it is not likely to be contagious as few fellow pupils are able to observe such acts. This decreased visibility also allows the teacher to exercise more personalistic means of control over misbehavior: There are fewer demands of equity and more time to handle problems on an individual basis. Although the teachers observed in this research tended to rely on the control forms associated with the predominant classroom activity – those using recitation relied on formal control sanctions whereas those using multitask activities exercised more individualized and personalistic controls – each teacher shifted control bases when utilizing another activity type. As the teachers faced different situations of group management, their exercise of authority differed accordingly. The task organization, then, by specifying the group management situation in a classroom, influences the type of control exercised by a teacher.

Moreover, classroom task organization also affected patterns in the allocation of special instructional assistance. Although all four teachers indicated that they provided the most assistance to pupils having the most difficulty, the teachers in the multitask classrooms were the only ones for whom this was true. The teachers who predominately used recitation relied on their top performers to contribute during recitations and serve as models for the rest of the class. These pupils received the most individual assistance. In the multitask classrooms, by contrast, there were few common tasks for the entire class; hence none of the children could become standards for the task activities. Pupils who did excel in a particular task were expected to help others or to work independently, leaving the teacher free to assist those pupils having the most difficulty. The development of an academic hierarchy only occurred in the recitation-organized classrooms, where the single task structure and comparative assessments of performance allowed for classroom ranking by achievement. This was shaped by the teachers' allocation of instructional assistance.

Peer associations also are influenced by the classroom task structure. In the recitation-dominated classrooms, friendship groupings began to form among children who were performing at similar levels. Because the structure of recitation makes task performance both visible and contingent on others' performances, pupils know one another's achievements and failures, become concerned about their relative achievements, and evaluate each other in terms of common performance criteria. The resulting academic stratification fosters competitive relations and stimulates within-achievement group associations. In the nonrecitation classrooms, by contrast, relative achievement level did not affect peer associations because task performance was less visible than in recitation, largely independent of others' performances, and noncomparable. The scope and fluidity of peer relations in these classrooms indicated that task performance was not an important factor in choosing friends. Moreover, differences in patterns of peer choices among the children who experienced different classroom task organizations indicate that cooperative and competitive peer relations are not necessarily linked to inherent personality characteristics of the children. Pupils who participated in competitive peer networks in their recitation-dominated third-grade class became less competitive and chose friends without regard for achievement level in the multitask-organized fourth-grade class. Likewise, the performance level of friends became an important factor after children had entered the recitation-dominated fourth-grade classroom, despite its unimportance the preceding year. To the extent that task performances are visible, comparable, and clearly linked to classroom rewards, children will choose friends on the basis of academic status.

In summary, a classroom's task organization specifies who interacts with whom as well as the context in which the interaction occurs. Differences in work organization affect the patterns of teacher-pupil and peer interaction that arise within a given task activity and within classrooms utilizing distinctive activity structures. In many ways, classrooms are like other work settings.[2] Classroom patterns of control, status differentiation, competition, cooperation, and supervision parallel those reported in a variety of group contexts. As work forms vary, so do basic patterns of social relations. Viewing classroom structure as an activity organization provides an important analytic tool for delineating the forces that shape social interaction within schools and for differentiating classroom patterns.

This activity structure perspective gives a new focus to studies of schooling processes. Generally, classroom research has suffered from "black box" designs and individualistic, personality models of behavior. Many studies measure only "inputs" and "outputs" without attempting to discover or assess processes that shape teacher and pupil behavior. Even when classroom behavior is observed, researchers emphasize the personal characteristics of the teachers and pupils – their attitudes and backgrounds – as prime determinants of action. Both approaches have contributed little to the understanding of schooling precisely because they ignore the fact that education is a social activity – its outcomes being influenced by its form of social organization. The analysis of classroom task organizations and of their effect on the development of social relationships discloses some of the contents of the educational "black box" and moves beyond simplistic models of behavior. It recognizes that all behavior is situated and, hence, influenced by the structural properties of the setting in which it occurs. By focusing on the organization of recurrent task activities, researchers can illuminate the variable conditions in which patterns of interaction develop and social relationships form, and trace their consequences explicitly.

Although the study reported in these pages is far from a definitive treatment of group life in classrooms, it demonstrates the fruitfulness of an activity structure analysis in school settings and examines some of the effects of variations in instructional organization. These effects are probably most visible at the elementary level where the child's proximal learning environment consists of a single classroom – one that can be classified and examined readily in terms of its use of several basic instructional forms. In secondary schools and colleges, the organization of instruction becomes much more complex and, hence, the unit for a task analysis may not be solely the internal organization of work groupings (classrooms). At this level, the study of activity structures might include the sequencing, interdependence, segmentation, and similarity among various work groups as well. Moreover, instructional activities themselves may exhibit more varied forms than recitation, class task, and multitask activities. For example, in high school and particularly in college, lectures and group discussions probably constitute distinct forms of work; in elementary schools, however, teachers rarely lecture or let children "discuss" without continually interrupting with questions, thus imposing recitation formats on both of these activity forms. Despite the complexity added by more differentiated work forms, an activity structure analysis should prove valuable to understanding social interaction at all levels of schooling. Schools are places where people work. The organization of work activities provides the context in which individuals interact and social relationships form. Therefore, a basic understanding of the social processes of schooling must take into account the ways in which task forms structure how individuals experience the learning environment.

7. Activity structures and learning: some implications

The value of the activity structure perspective is not limited only to the analysis of patterns of interaction within classrooms. It also may provide an important model for studying learning – one that not only fills the educational "black box" but explicitly links social processes to schooling outcomes. In addition to the pedagogical effects that derive from content characteristics of instructional activities, the classroom social relationships that result from particular instructional organizations may influence pupil achievement and socialization directly. The research reported in the preceding chapters was not designed to assess the socialization outcomes of differences in classroom instructional organization, and there are no data that allow for a direct analysis of this concern. But the examination of activity structures and their effects does suggest several possible models for assessing the consequences of certain structural arrangements for learning.

Instructional organization and achievement

There are two possible effects of classroom instructional organization on pupil achievement. First, pupil achievement may be influenced by the effect task organization has on the allocation of individualized teacher assistance (see Chapter 4). Because one of the most important aspects of a teacher's skill is the ability to handle fluctuations in pupils' responses to instruction (Bidwell, 1965), a teacher must be able to allocate time for individual assistance when pupils need additional help. The teacher who uses multitask activities is able to provide individual assistance when necessary. This task organization frees a teacher from constant control over instructional activities and allows him to give the most assistance to pupils having trouble. Recitation, however, gives the teacher few opportunities to provide individual assistance, and when assistance is given, the top achievers receive a disproportionately high share. The task organization of a classroom, then, may inhibit or enhance a teacher's ability to supply special individualized assistance to some pupils. Hence pupil achievement may be influenced by the task organization of a classroom through the task activity's effect on teacher assistance patterns.

A second way the task organization of a classroom may influence pupil achievement is in its effect on teacher authority. Bidwell has argued that a teacher must establish a relationship of trust between himself and his pupils in order to overcome the potentially hostile situation of control that may result from students' involuntary recruitment into schools. "Student trust in teachers is of the greatest importance in teaching as it generates those affective bonds between teachers and students . . . that generate in students motivation to learn (whatever the content to be learned) independently of teacher demands for compliance" (Bidwell, 1970, p. 50). Therefore, a teacher seemingly cannot rely on the authority of office to control pupils; personal bonds of trust and rapport are necessary for gaining pupil compliance and promoting learning within a classroom.

In his theoretical treatment of teacher authority and student unrest, Spady (1974) further elaborates the importance of trust for promoting achievement. He argues that a teacher cannot simply rely on the exercise of power; this results in a confrontation between teacher demands and pupil desires, and can cause pupil alienation. To provide a conducive learning environment, the teacher must gain the willing compliance of his pupils. Spady notes that a teacher accomplishes this by showing that he is concerned about his pupils' welfare and by demonstrating his ability to provide stimulating learning tasks. Spady, then, hypothesizes two major dimensions of teacher authority, empathy and expertise. A teacher who can evoke excitement in the curriculum, show concern for his pupils, and demonstrate expertise in his teaching will be able to establish the rapport necessary to gain willing compliance from his pupils and, hence, provide a classroom situation that maximally stimulates learning.

Teachers who rely primarily on the exercise of formal, institutional authority will not be able to develop affective bonds that promote willing compliance, the motivation to learn, and achievement among their pupils. Achievement, then, may be linked to the type of authority exercised by a teacher (though no empirical examination of this hypothesis has been made).

In their arguments, Bidwell and Spady seem to assume that a teacher's

ability to establish trust in and rapport with pupils is primarily a consequence of the teacher's individual characteristics. Spady, in particular,
indicates that teachers who have both a high degree of empathy toward
their pupils and a high level of subject matter and pedagogical expertise
should be the most effective. However, teacher authority may not be
solely a consequence of teacher personality; it also results from the
activity structure that is utilized within the classroom.

For example, the ability to demonstrate pedagogical and subject
matter competence did not seem to vary among the teachers studied
in this research. Their pupils considered them to be "good" teachers.
However, pupil perceptions of teacher rapport varied significantly. The
two recitation-oriented teachers, Ms. Hunt and Ms. Field, were considered less friendly and warm than the two multitask-oriented teachers,
Mr. Stone and Ms. Park. In comparing their teachers, the fourth-grade
children who had either Stone and Field or Hunt and Park noted substantial differences.

[From pupil interviews]

Eliza: Ms. Hunt is much more stricter than Ms. Park. Ms. Park lets
you do more things. In Ms. Hunt's room you just sit and do a lot
of work.
Ellen: Ms. Hunt wasn't much fun. She never did anything with us,
except lead some clapping and singing games sometimes.
Eliza: Yeah, Ms. Park is always doing stuff with us.

David: Ms. Field seems further away [than Mr. Stone].
Charles: You can't get to know Ms. Field as well. She never does
anything with us.

Bill: I like Mr. Stone much better. He associated with us.
Mike: They have taught me about the same amount of work. But
they are so different. Ms. Field doesn't play ball with us, for one.
Mr. Stone is not as strict. Though, when he blew up, he really did.
Bill: So does Ms. Field.
Mike: Yeah, just about everyday.

Lisa: I like Mr. Stone because he came to our special classes with us
and did it [projects] with us, too. If you needed him he was right
there.

Children who remained in classrooms where the task structure paralleled their previous year's experience did not mention any differences between their teachers, except some minor personal differences like hair color, age, smile, and singing voice.

Although both Hunt and Field expressed concern for their pupils and were able to provide as sympathetic treatment of children as Stone and Park, two aspects of the task organization of their classroom seemed to inhibit the development of strong affective bonds between them and their pupils. First, both Hunt and Field primarily used short impartial commands (desists) to sanction misbehaving children. This method is the most appropriate one for a recitation format as it allows the recitation to continue with minimal interruption (see Chapter 4). Park and Stone by contrast, usually talked with the misbehaving child, explaining why the conduct was inappropriate and suggesting proper behavior. The multitask setting allows for this personal control because the teacher is not the leader of the instructional activity: The class can proceed while the teacher is handling one child individually. When Stone and Park used recitation in their classrooms, they were not able to treat personally every behavior problem, and they also relied on desists to sanction misbehavior. Likewise, Hunt and Field used substantially more personal methods of control (rather than desists) during multitask activities in their classrooms. The predominance of one type of instructional task, however, seemed to have a contextual effect: Recitation-dominated classrooms with their relatively high levels of desists and fewer personalized controls seemed to decrease the opportunities for the development of strong, affective teacher-pupil bonds.

Second, since the recitation format places a teacher in full control over the activity, recitation teachers rarely become involved in the activity, as participants, with their pupils. An important quality of friendliness mentioned previously by most of Stone's and Park's pupils was teacher participation in task activities with the class. This participation seemed to allow these two teachers to establish much more rapport with their pupils than if they had been only directors of activity. Hunt and Field, however, rarely became involved in classroom task activities as participants; their primary role was that of leader of the recitation.

Therefore, it was not that Hunt and Field were personally less empathic than Stone and Park; rather, the task organization of these classrooms influenced the method of control and the extent of teacher involvement in task activities, which, in turn, affected the development of empathic relationships.

Unfortunately, data collected in this research cannot test the relationship among task organization, teacher authority, and pupil achievement. However, if Bidwell and Spady are correct in their hypotheses that the degree of trust and rapport in the teacher-pupil relationship affects pupil achievement, the task organization may affect pupil achievement, independent of pedagogical differences in the task types. Seemingly, the multitask organization, which enhances a teacher's opportunity to develop rapport with the pupils, may be more conducive to pupil achievement than recitation. Of course, this is not to imply that recitation is inappropriate for instruction. Task types have direct pedagogical effects related to the transmission of curriculum content, apart from differences in their interactional form. However, these consequences must be considered jointly. Future research on factors influencing pupil achievement should take into account the importance of this task organization effect on teacher authority.

Instructional organization and moral socialization

In addition to achievement effects, moral socialization outcomes may derive from the organization of classroom task activities. For example, others already have argued that task experience is an important source of attitudes and norms. In relation to schools, Dreeben (1968) contends that children learn norms of independence, achievement, universalism, and specificity from the tasks they are expected to do in school. He points out that the structural arrangements resulting from having a large number of similar-aged children and a relatively small number of teachers create situations in which children learn to act alone, accept universalistic achievement criteria when their work is evaluated, and evaluate others in terms of their positions in the school structure (e.g., as another fourth grader). The process by which these norms are instilled is one of instrumental reinforcement and generalization. Following Breer and Locke's (1965) formulation of task experience as a sources of attitudes, Dreeben argues that children develop task-specific norms (i.e., how one should do a task) by successfully completing recurrent tasks. Task-specific norms are generalized to similar tasks and then to a variety of other situations as these norms are used successfully. General principles of conduct, therefore, emerge from specific recurrent task experiences provided in schools.[1]

Although Dreeben does not explore the consequences of within-school variations in task experience on socialization, his general framework can be used to examine differences in norm learning outcomes among children who receive diverse classroom task experiences. That is, just as family and school differ in the activities they provide children and, hence, in the norm learning outcomes that result, classrooms that offer different task experiences may induce different moral socialization outcomes. Although the research presented here did not analyze the effect of classroom task organization on moral socialization, it does provide a first step toward an examination of this relationship.

It has been shown that classroom instructional activities can entail different patterns of task behavior. Recitation, for example, requires children to pay attention to the teacher, wait to be recognized before speaking, and for the most part not interact with fellow pupils. As Jackson (1968) pointed out, recitation teaches children to be patient, act alone, and defer to teacher authority. By contrast, multitask activities may teach children to be cooperative and self-directed because these activities require children to work together and organize their own projects without the constant supervision of the teacher. Classrooms organized around different task activities, then, may foster the development of different task-specific norms: Children from recitation-organized classrooms may be more independent (in the sense of acting alone) and less self-directed and cooperative than children from multitask-organized classrooms. By successfully coping with the most frequent classroom tasks, children may generalize these task-specific norms to other situations.

There is some indication of this occurring among the Harper School children. Teachers of the special classes noted that children from the recitation-dominated classrooms were more capable of following teacher directions but less self-directed and cooperative in small work groups than the children from the multitask classrooms. For example, the science teacher repeatedly complained that Stone's pupils were unable to come into her room and sit quietly until she gave instructions. According to her, "They just come running in – into everything I've put out. All of them want to begin immediately; doing their own thing. They're not like Ms. Hunt's class. Her control really shows up in the way they behave in my room." Yet this teacher did note that Stone's pupils were much more cooperative when working on projects in assigned groups – groups that usually separated the children from existing classroom friendship networks. In addition, the art teacher commented that Stone's and Park's children generally were more open to exploring "new forms of expression" than pupils from Hunt's and Field's classes. He explained, "It's probably due to their [the teachers'] styles. Park and Stone encourage their kids to try their own ideas. Bill is a good example. Last year [while in Mr. Stone's class] he was one of my best innovators. Not as good on technique as Terry, but OK. This year [in Ms. Field's class] all he asks for is directions – won't try anything on his own." These examples seem to illustrate that task behavior learned in the regular classroom transferred to other classes. It is reasonable to hypothesize that if children have *consistent* classroom task experiences for a number of years, classroom task behavior and the task-specific norms that derive from them may generalize to other situations, thus becoming general principles for conduct. Although the children of Harper School seem very adaptable to their classroom task structure from year to year and the school structure almost guarantees that children will experience different classroom task organizations across the years, the effect of consistent task experience on norm generalization is an empirical question – both in the sense of identifying the extent of consistency in children's schooling experiences over time and in the effect that varying degrees of consistency have on norm learning.

These ideas suggest that research on the moral socialization consequences of schooling must take into account the task organization of classrooms. Many questions then arise: What are the normative outcomes of classroom tasks? How different are children's classroom task experiences over several years; are there individual variations as children progress through school, or do schools or school districts vary in terms of the types of task organizations they provide? What effect does the length of participation in a particular task organization have on norm generalization? Are there crucial periods in a child's development that make exposure to a particular task organization more influential on normative outcomes than others? To understand moral socialization, then, research must examine variations in the content and timing of children's participation in classrooms with different or consistent instructional organizations.

An analysis of work in a setting, therefore, discloses the basic link between organizational structure and learning. After all, socialization is a process of social interaction. The nature of recurrent task activities shapes this process by setting the context in which interpersonal assessments occur and social relationships form.

Appendix A. Interview schedules

Pupil interview

Fourth-grade children

Introduction: As you know I've been observing in your classrooms this year and last year. I have some ideas of what third and fourth graders like to do, but I thought that I should find out what you think. What kinds of things do you like or dislike in school?

A. What are the differences between last year and this year?
    Probes:
    What things do you like to do or dislike?
    What did you like about last year that you don't do this year?
    What things do you like this year that you didn't do last year?

B. How does Mr. Stone (or, Ms. Hunt) compare to Ms. Park (or, Ms. Field)?
    Probes:
    How are they the same?
    How are they different?
    Which one do you like better?

C. If you could tell your teacher what to do or change in your class what would you tell her?

D. Do you like the kids in your class this year?
    Probes:
    Who are your best friends?
    Are the kids different from last year's class?
    Who were your best friends last year?

If you could change where you sit, where would you move?
Who are the smartest kids? Why?
Which kids cause the most trouble? Why?

Teacher interview

Teacher – before beginning of school year

A. Could you give me an idea of your plans for this year?
    Probes:
    Schedules of classes.
    Special curriculum materials or programs to be used.

B. What do you expect with this new group of pupils?
    Probes:
    Have you looked at their records?
    What do you look for the first day?

C. Are you planning to do anything different from last year?
    Probes:
    Why?

D. From the list of last year's pupils would you give a brief descrip-
    tion of each child's academic strengths and weakness and any
    behavior problems? What would you predict for these pupils
    in the fourth grade? [This question was for the third-grade
    teachers only.]

Teacher – periodically during the school year

A. From this list of your pupils, how would you rate each child's
    academic performance?
    Probes:
    Subject matter variation.
    Do you think this child is working up to his (her) potential?

B. What are some of the behavior problems or adjustment problems
    of these children?

Appendix B. Supplementary tables

Table B.1. *Weekly summary of peer group composition: Ms. Field's classroom*

| | Number of | | | Percent of groups homogeneous by | | | | | |
Week	Groups	Changes	Children not in groups	Sex	Race	Neighborhood	Classmates last year	Seatmates	Achievement level
1	8	—	2	100	63	50	63	100	38
2	8	1	2	100	63	50	63	100	38
3									
4	7	5	3	100	71	58	43	85	58
5	6	2	[3]	100	67	50	[0]	83	67
6									
7	7	1	2	100	43	43	14	85	85
8	7	2	3	100	58	43	14	100	100
9									
10									
11									
12	[8]	[4]	[1]	100	[38]	[50]	[25]	100	[75]
13									
14	[8]	3	[1]	100	[38]	[50]	[25]	100	[75]
15									
16									
17									
18									
19									
20	7	3	3	100	58	58	14	100	85
21									

Note: This table indicates only the groups of children who *worked* together. Changes from work and play groupings are in brackets. Compare Table 5.1.

105

Table B.2. *Weekly summary of peer group composition: Ms. Field's classroom*

Week	Number of			Percent of groups homogeneous by					
	Groups	Changes	Children not in groups	Sex	Race	Neighborhood	Classmates last year	Seatmates	Achievement level
1	8	—	2	100	63	50	63	100	38
2	8	1	[0]	100	63	50	[50]	100	38
3									
4	7	5	3	100	[58]	58	[29]	[71]	[43]
5	[7]	2	[1]	100	[58]	[58]	[29]	[71]	[58]
6									
7	7	1	[1]	100	43	43	14	85	85
8	7	2	[1]	[85]	58	43	14	[85]	[85]
9									
10									
11									
12	7	3	[0]	100	[29]	[43]	29	[85]	71
13									
14	7	3	[0]	100	[29]	[43]	29	[85]	71
15									
16									
17									
18									
19									
20	7	3	3	100	58	58	14	100	85
21									

Note: This table indicates only the groups of children who *played* together. Changes from work and play groupings are in brackets. Compare Table 5.1.

Table B.3. *Weekly summary of peer group composition: Ms. Park's classroom*

Week	Number of		Children not in groups	Percent of groups homogeneous by					
	Groups	Changes		Sex	Race	Neighborhood	Classmates last year	Seatmates	Achievement level
1	7	—	[2]	100	58	29	71	100	14
1	5	6	1	100	20	20	0	100	0
2									
3	[7]	5	1	100	[38]	[43]	[29]	[86]	[14]
4	7	3	1	100	29	58	43	100	14
5									
6	6	3	1	100	50	33	17	100	0
7									
8	[6]	4	0	100	[33]	[17]	[33]	[83]	[17]
9									
10	5	6	4	100	40	40	20	100	20
11									
12	[6]	3	3	100	[50]	[50]	[50]	[83]	[17]
13									
14	7	2	[1]	86	58	43	14	100	43
15									
16	7	2	3	100	58	58	43	100	14
17									
18									
19	7	3	1	100	29	58	43	100	14
20	7	3	1	100	71	58	43	100	14
21									

Note: This table indicates only the groups of children who *played* together. Changes from work and play groupings are in brackets. Compare Table 5.4.

Table B.4. *Weekly summary of peer group composition: Mr. Stone's classroom*

| Week | Number of | | | Percent of groups homogeneous by | | | | | |
	Groups	Changes	Children not in groups	Sex	Race	Neighborhood	Classmates last year	Seatmates	Achievement level
1	7	–	4	100	29	43	86	100	29
2	7	4	2	100	29	43	58	100	29
3	8	6	3	100	50	75	50	87	25
4									
5									
6	8	6	4	100	63	75	38	100	38
7									
8	8	4	6	100	38	63	38	100	38
9	8	2	5	100	38	63	38	100	38
10	8	1	4	100	38	63	38	100	38
11									
12	7	8	5	100	43	71	29	100	29
13									
14	7	2	6	100	43	71	29	100	29
15									
16	9	7	[2]	[89]	33	78	22	100	44
17									
18									
19	7	2	4	86	58	71	29	100	29
20	9	4	3	100	67	78	44	100	33
21									

Note: This table indicates only the groups of children who *worked* together. Changes from work and play groupings are in brackets. Compare Table 5.3.

Table B.5. *Weekly summary of peer group composition: Mr. Stone's classroom*

	Number of			Percent of groups homogeneous by					
Week	Groups	Changes	Children not in groups	Sex	Race	Neighborhood	Classmates last year	Seatmates	Achievement level
1	7	—	[3]	100	[14]	43	86	[86]	29
2	[6]	4	2	100	[17]	[50]	[33]	[83]	[17]
3	[9]	6	[1]	100	[44]	[67]	[44]	[78]	[33]
4									
5									
6	8	6	4	100	63	75	38	100	38
7									
8	8	4	[4]	100	38	63	[25]	[75]	[25]
9	8	2	5	100	38	63	38	100	38
10	8	1	4	100	38	63	38	100	38
11									
12	7	8	5	100	43	71	29	100	29
13									
14	7	2	[4]	100	43	71	[0]	[71]	[14]
15									
16	[7]	[6]	[3]	100	[43]	[86]	[14]	[86]	[29]
17									
18									
19	7	2	4	86	58	71	29	100	29
20	9	4	3	100	67	78	44	100	33
21									

Note: This table indicates only the groups of children who *played* together. Changes from work and play groups are in brackets. Compare Table 5.3.

Table B.6. *Weekly summary of peer group composition: Ms. Hunt's classroom*

Week	Number of		Children not in groups	Percent of groups homogeneous by					
	Groups	Changes		Sex	Race	Neighborhood	Classmates last year	Seatmates	Achievement level
1	9	—	0	100	67	34	78	100	11
2									
3	9	5	3	100	45	45	33	100	33
4									
5									
6									
7									
8									
9									
10	10	4	1	100	50	50	30	90	60
11									
12	7	5	4	100	29	43	14	100	71
13									
14	7	1	[2]	100	[14]	[29]	14	[85]	[58]
15									
16									
17									
18									
19									
20									
21									

Note: This table indicates only the groups of children who *played* together. Changes from work and play groupings are in brackets. Compare Table 5.2.

110

Table B.7. *Work and play group composition by achievement mix: Ms. Field's classroom*

Week	Number of groups	Achievement level composition						
		1	2	3	1 & 2	1 & 3	2 & 3	1, 2 & 3
1	8	1	1		4	1		1
2	8	2	1		4	1		
3								
4	7	2	2		1	1	1	
5	6	3	1		1		1	
6								
7	7	3	2	1	1			
8	7	3	3	1				
9								
10								
11								
12	7	2	2	1	2			
13								
14	7	2	2	1	2			
15								
16								
17								
18								
19								
20	7	3	2	1	1			
21								

Note: Achievement levels denoted by: (1) top performers, (2) average performers, and (3) poor performers.

111

Table B.8. *Work and play group composition by achievement mix: Ms. Hunt's classroom*

Week	Number of groups	Achievement level composition						
		1	2	3	1 & 2	1 & 3	2 & 3	1, 2 & 3
1	9			1	3	1	2	2
2								
3	9	1	1	1	1	1	3	1
4								
5								
6								
7								
8								
9								
10	10	1	2	3	2	1	1	
11								
12	7	2	1	2	1	1		
13								
14	7	2	1	2	1	1		
15								
16								
17								
18								
19								
20								
21								

Note: Achievement levels denoted by: (1) top performers, (2) average performers, and (3) poor performers.

Table B.9. *Work and play group composition by achievement mix: Mr. Stone's classroom*

Week	Number of groups	Achievement level composition						
		1	2	3	1 & 2	1 & 3	2 & 3	1, 2 & 3
1	7	1		1	2		1	2
2	7	1		1	2		1	2
3	8	1		1		2	2	2
4								
5								
6	8	2		1	2	1	1	1
7								
8	8	1	2	3	2			
9	8	1	2	3	2			
10	8	1	2	2	2	1		
11								
12	7	1	1		2	1	2	
13								
14	7	1		1	2	2	1	
15								
16	9	2		2	2	1	2	
17								
18								
19	7	1		1	2	1	1	1
20	9	2		1	2	1	2	1
21								

Note: Achievement levels denoted by: (1) top performers, (2) average performers, and (3) poor performers.

Table B.10. *Work and play group composition by achievement mix: Ms. Park's classroom*

Week	Number of groups	Achievement level composition						
		1	2	3	1 & 2	1 & 3	2 & 3	1, 2 & 3
1	7	1			2		3	1
1	5				1	1	1	2
2								
3	8	1	1		2	2	2	
4	7		1		3	2	1	
5								
6	6				3		2	1
7								
8	7		1	1	2	1	1	1
9								
10	5	1			1	1	1	1
11								
12	7	1			3		3	
13								
14	7	1	1	1	3		1	
15								
16	7	1			2	1	3	
17								
18								
19	7	1			3	2	1	
20	7	1			3		2	1
21								

Note: Achievement levels denoted by: (1) top performers, (2) average performers, and (3) poor performers.

114

Notes

Chapter 1. Introduction

1 In part, this lack of attention to emergent aspects of social relationships is a function of the behaviorists' research methodology. Short observation periods in which subjects' behaviors are coded into preset, standardized categories preclude the examination of emergent phenomena.

2 Classroom task activities shall refer to those projects that children are expected to perform as part of the instructional enterprise in a classroom. Others have attempted to define task in various ways: Thibaut and Kelly (1959, p. 150) and Breer and Locke have referred to a task as "a complex of stimuli upon which the individual performs certain operations in order to achieve certain outcomes" (Breer and Locke, 1965, p. 9). However, this definition has not really improved on Ryan's (1958) notion that a task is merely what an individual is doing. In a sense, every action has task components. This research is not intended to define the component parts of all acts, but rather to analyze how particular instructional activities are organized.

Chapter 2. The setting and study design

1 All names are fictitious.

2 Ms. Hunt had twenty-five new pupils. Mr. Stone had twenty-six new pupils.

3 See Lofland, 1971, pp. 117–33, for a description of data handling in field research.

4 The researcher's purpose was first described to the teachers as an interest in peer relations. A full explanation was made when the study was discussed at the end of the year.

Chapter 3. Four classrooms

1 The following description is based only on data collected during the second year of observations. However, many of the same patterns occurred the preceding year.

2 All classes in this elementary school ate lunch as a group in their own rooms. There were no special lunchrooms.

3 The following description is based only on data collected during the second year of observations. However, many of the same patterns occurred the preceding year.

Chapter 4. The teacher-pupil relationship

1 This definition of desist deviates from its standard usage. Throughout this book, desist (when used as a noun) will mean a quick command to stop a behavior or activity that violates classroom rules. Kounin (1970, p. 2) has set the precedent for such usage by defining desist as "a teacher's doing something to stop a misbehavior."

2 Ms. Hunt averaged 24 desists per 100 minutes, and Mr. Stone averaged 7.

3 For examples see White and Lippitt (1962) and Gordon and Adler (1963).

4 The research reported here was not designed to test whether classroom task organization is a better predictor of control usage than personality factors. The initial choice of tasks may reflect a teacher's predilection for certain types of control. However, once chosen, the exigencies of the task structure seem to influence a teacher's control behavior. Moreover, although teachers often have considerable autonomy over the content of classroom lessons, supervisors or prescribed curriculum materials may specify methods of instruction (e.g., several teachers have reported that they were "forced" to use recitation because they were required to teach a specific number of pages each week from a standard text despite their personal preferences for other instructional methods).

5 On the importance of trust and goodwill in the classroom, see Bidwell (1970) and Dreeben (1968).

6 Kounin (1970) has given some excellent examples of teachers' use of desists.

7 Hunt rarely used multitask activities during this year, and when she did, she tended to control the whole class rather than circulate from group to group. Note her high desist rate (shown in Table 4.1) even during the multitask activities.

8 The amount of teacher assistance each pupil received is impossible to calculate accurately from the observation notes, because time periods were only recorded in approximately five-minute segments.

9 It should be noted that all six classrooms were balanced in terms of the pupils' past achievements and test scores.

Chapter 5. Peer relations

1 Parents' occupational statuses were not significantly different, to indicate social class differences in classroom peer relations often observed by others (e.g., Neugarten, 1942; Dahlke, 1953; Lippitt and Gold, 1959; Schmuck, 1962).

2 A child's performance level was indicated by classroom teacher ratings.

Chapter 6. The impact of task organization

1 An interesting study might involve tracing certain teacher background variables and their effect on teachers' choices of task activities; variables such as age, sex, training, experience, and social class origins may influence the choice of task structure.

2 This is not to imply the crude "school as factory" metaphor. Even though members of industrial work groups and classrooms do engage in task activities, many other aspects of these organizations are different. Members of industrial work groups generally produce a tangible product; their membership is voluntary; workers vary in age and job experience; the duration of the work group is usually longer than any worker's membership in it; and rewards are generally in the form of wages. Children in school, by contrast, seldom produce tangible products (the primary "products" of the school being technical and moral socialization); their membership is involuntary; children generally are grouped by age; classroom groups typically last only one year, with most children beginning and ending their membership at the same time; and rewards are often tangible (praise) or symbolic (grades). Yet, despite these differences, similar patterns of group relations emerge when similar forms of work are observed.

Chapter 7. Activity structures and learning: some implications

1 Of course, this is not to say that schools are the only setting where children have recurrent task experiences. Dreeben argues that settings differ in their normative consequences because differences in structural arrangements create different recurrent tasks.

References

Becker, Howard S. Problems of proof and inference in participant observation. *American Sociological Review*, 1958, *23*, 652–60.

Bidwell, Charles E. The school as a formal organization. In J. G. March (ed.), *Handbook of Organizations*. Chicago: Rand McNally, 1965. Pp. 972–1022.

Students and schools: some observations on client trust in client-serving organizations. In W. R. Rosengren and M. Lefton (eds.), *Organizations and Clients*. Columbus, Ohio: Merrill, 1970.

Schooling and socialization for moral commitment. *Interchange*, 1972, *3*, 1–27.

Blau, Peter M. *The Dynamics of Bureaucracy*. Chicago: University of Chicago Press, 1965.

Boocock, Sarane S. *An Introduction to the Sociology of Learning*. Boston: Houghton Mifflin, 1972.

Borgatta, Edgar F., and R. F. Bales. Task and accumulation of experience as factors in the interaction of small groups. *Sociometry*, 1953, *16*, 239–52.

Bossert, Steven T. School sociologist/specialist on learning environments: some thoughts on possible models. In A. J. Schwartz (ed.), "Proceedings of the National Invitational Conference on School Sociologists." Los Angeles: University of Southern California, School of Education, 1975.

Breer, Paul E., and Edwin A. Locke. *Task Experience as a Source of Attitudes*. Homewood, Ill.: Dorsey Press, 1965.

Breton, Yvan. A comparative study of work groups in an eastern Canadian peasant fishing community: bilateral kinship and adaptive processes. *Ethnology*, 1973, *12*, 393–418.

Brophy, J., and T. Good. *Teacher-Student Relationships: Causes and Consequences*. New York: Holt, 1974.

Bush, R. N. *The Teacher-Pupil Relationship*. New York: Prentice-Hall, 1954.

Dahlke, H. O. Determinants of sociometric relations among children in elementary school. *Sociometry*, 1953, *16*, 327–38.

Dreeben, Robert. *On What Is Learned in School*. Reading, Mass.: Addison-Wesley, 1968.

Durkheim, E. *Moral Education*. Glencoe, Ill.: Free Press, 1961.

Flanders, Ned A. *Teacher Influence, Pupil Attitudes and Achievements*. Office of Education, Cooperative Research Monograph No. 12, 1960.

Glaser, Barney G., and Anselm L. Strauss. *The Discovery of Grounded Theory*. Chicago: Aldine, 1967.

Gordon, C. W. *The Social System of the High School*. Glencoe, Ill.: Free Press, 1957.

Gordon, C. W., and L. M. Adler. "Dimensions of Teacher Leadership in Classroom Social Systems." Los Angeles: University of California, Department of Education, 1963. (Mimeographed)

Grann, L. R. The relationship between academic achievement of pupils and the social structure of the classroom. *Rural Sociology*, 1956, *21*, 179–80.

Grolund, Norman E. Relationship between sociometric status of pupils and teachers' preferences for or against having them in class. *Sociometry*, 1953, *16*, 142–50.

Gump, Paul V. "The Classroom Behavior Setting." Washington, D.C.: Office of Education, 1967.

Gump, Paul V., and B. Sutton-Smith. Activity-setting and social interaction. *American Journal of Orthopsychiatry*, 1955, *25*, 755–60.

Hoetker, James, and W. P. Ahlbrand, Jr. The persistence of the recitation. *American Educational Research Journal*, 1969, *6*, 145–67.

Homans, George C. *The Human Group*. New York: Harcourt, Brace, 1950.

Hughes, Marie M. "Assessment of the Quality of Teaching in Elementary Schools." Washington, D.C.: Office of Education, 1959.

Jackson, Philip W. *Life in Classrooms*. New York: Holt, 1968.

Kounin, Jacob S. *Discipline and Group Management in Classrooms*. New York: Holt, 1970.

Kowatrakul, Surang. Some behaviors of elementary school children related to classroom activities and subject areas. *Journal of Educational Psychology*, 1959, *50*, 121–8.

Lewin, K., R. Lippitt, and R. K. White. Patterns of aggressive behavior in three "social climates." *Journal of Social Psychology*, 1939, *10*, 271–99.

Lippitt, R., and M. Gold. Classroom social structure as a mental health problem. *Journal of Social Issues*, 1959, *15*, 40–9.

Lippitt, R., and R. K. White. Leader behavior and member reaction in three "social climates." In D. Cartwright and A. Zander (eds.), *Group Dynamics*. Evanston, Ill.: Row, Peterson, 1962. Pp. 527–52.

Lofland, John. *Analyzing Social Settings*. Belmont, Ca.: Wadsworth, 1971.

Lortie, Dan C. *School Teacher*. Chicago: University of Chicago Press, 1975.

Mead, George Herbert. *Mind, Self and Society*. Chicago: University of Chicago Press, 1934.

Medley, D. M., and H. E. Mitzel. Measuring classroom behavior by systematic observation. In N. L. Gage (ed.), *Handbook of Research on Teaching*. Chicago: Rand McNally, 1963.

Miller, L. K., and R. L. Hamblin. Interdependence, differential rewarding, and productivity. *American Sociological Review*, 1963, *28*, 768–78.

Neugarten, Bernice. Social class and friendship among school children. *American Journal of Sociology*, 1942, *51*, 305–13.

Parsons, T. The school as a social system. *Harvard Educational Review*, 1959, *29*, 297–318.

Rist, Ray C. Student social class and teacher expectations. *Harvard Educational Review*, 1970, *40*, 411–51.

Roy, D. Quota restriction and goldbricking in a machine shop. *American Journal of Sociology*, 1952, *47*, 427–42.

Ryan, T. A. Drives, tasks and the initiation of behavior. *American Journal of Psychology*, 1958, *71*, 74–93.

Sayles, Leonard R. *Behavior of Industrial Work Groups*. New York: Wiley, 1958.

Schmuck, R. Sociometric status and utilization of academic abilities. *Merrill-Palmer Quarterly*, 1962, *8*, 165–72.

Shils, Edward. Primary groups in the army. In R. K. Merton and P. F. Lazarsfeld (eds.), *Continuities in Social Research*. Glencoe, Ill.: Free Press, 1950. Pp. 16–37.

Simon, A., and E. Boyer (eds.). *Mirrors for Behavior*. Philadelphia: Research for Better Schools, 1970.

Spady, William G. The authority system of the school and student unrest: a theoretical exploration. In C. W. Gordon (ed.), *Uses of the Sociology of Education*. Chicago: National Society for the Study of Education, 1974. Pp. 36–77.

Stern, G. C. Environments for learning. In N. Stanford (ed.), *The American College*. New York: Wiley, 1962.

Street, David, R. Vinter, and C. Perrow. *Organization for Treatment*. New York: Free Press, 1966.

Thibaut, John W., and H. H. Kelly. *The Social Psychology of Groups*. New York: Wiley, 1959.

Waller, Willard. *The Sociology of Teaching*. New York: Wiley, 1932.

Weber, Max. *The Theory of Social and Economic Organization*. New York: Oxford University Press, 1947.

Wheeler, Stanton. The structure of formally organized socialization settings. In O. Brim and S. Wheeler, *Socialization after Childhood*. New York: John Wiley, 1966. Pp. 53-116.

Woodward, J. *Management and Technology*. London: Her Majesty's Stationery Office, 1958.